flow

flow

FicSci 01

Edited by
Mehita Iqani and Wamuwi Mbao

AFRICAN
MINDS

Published in 2023 by African Minds
4 Eccleston Place, Somerset West, 7130, Cape Town, South Africa
info@africanminds.org.za | www.africanminds.org.za

ISBN (paper): 978-1-928502-73-9
eBook edition: 978-1-928502-74-6
ePub edition: 978-1-928502-75-3

Copies of this book are available for free download at: www.africanminds.org.za

ORDERS:
African Minds
Email: info@africanminds.org.za

To order printed books from outside Africa, please contact:
African Books Collective
PO Box 721, Oxford OX1 9EN, UK
Email: orders@africanbookscollective.com

Table of Contents

Acknowledgements

FicSci is a not-for-profit academic research project that aims to produce and support experimental interdisciplinary encounters between science and creative writing.

It is organised by the South African Research Chair in Science Communication and funded under the auspices of the National Research Foundation of South Africa. FicSci is a workshop convened by Prof. Mehita Iqani and Dr Wamuwi Mbao. For each workshop we invite a chosen scientist specialist to share their research. We select writers through a competitive application process.

We are very grateful to Prof. Malebogo Ngoepe for sharing her knowledge and time for FicSci 01. We thank Fumani Jwara for invaluable communications and logistical support on the project.

FicSci 01 was hosted at the Mont Fleur conference centre in the Blaauwklippen valley. We thank our hosts for the excellent food, blazing fires, and conducive writing environment.

This anthology is made available in its e-print version for free download to reach the widest audience. It is licenced under Creative Commons.

1

Notes from an Invited Scientist

Malebogo Ngoepe

"I need to ask a question that's really out there," the writer began.

"If we keep replacing the human heart, could people live in perpetuity?"

This, and countless other questions that never feature at my regular July conferences, interrupted my default flow of ideas. In the lighthearted moments in the science conferences and seminars I usually attend, the realities of methodological limitations, constrained budgets and societal relevance quickly drown out the necessary pleasure of w(a/o)ndering.

The questions felt like an invitation to follow streamlines directed by the writers' minds. Much like the trajectory of a fluid particle in flow, some questions took us along gentle, laminar paths, while others enabled us to marvel at the beauty of chaos, turbulence and randomness. Resolution's vacation of the driver's seat meant that we were freer to travel.

The first conversation was riveted around blood flow and blood clotting in the human body. Blood flow transports nutrients, oxygen and other substances around the body. Clotting normally serves a protective function that maintains the integrity of the blood vessels, which are the conduits through which blood flows. Disruption to the careful balance that regulates the clotting process can have catastrophic effects for flow, much like a mistimed stop-go control.

The second conversation explored human curly scalp hairs. We discussed the idea that every single hair runs on a unique alarm clock that determines whether it is growing or resting. We also explored the idea of hair fibres possessing various forms of memory. For example, they have biochemical memory which enables them to remember all meals, stressful events and hormonal changes. They also have mechanical memory which facilitates remembrance of their original physical shape, thanks to hydrogen bonds.

The third conversation focused on the development of a new heart attack therapy. Many of the existing therapies are designed to slow the time to inevitable heart failure. In an attempt to stimulate the regenerative capacity of the heart, various gels are being explored, with a view to injecting them into the injured part of the heart. Setbacks to this technology include poor retention of the injected media, given the vigorous pumping action of the heart. Even when injured. Which takes us back to the opening question ...

I seem to recall being asked whether the heart or the brain was the regulatory centre for humans, in this particular hypothetical exploration. "Definitely the heart," I explained. I quickly wandered over to motor vehicles, which seemed like similar enough organisms, at the time, given the engine, pump, pipes, ability to consume and ability to make noises of various frequencies. If you changed the engine and nothing else, the other parts would eventually fail because materials wear over time. "You can change those parts too," I said. So if you keep modifying various parts under the shell, at which point does it cease to be the original vehicle?

With that in mind, I continue to wonder about the consistently high levels of oxygen and speeds of flow that could be sustained infinitely. Would each individual cell continue to pay ultimate allegiance to its own alarm clock, while routinely checking in with neighbour cells to ensure some level of societal cohesion? Or would the conditions give sufficiently different chemo-mechano-biological cues to cell society, thereby allowing individual cells to collectively suspend disbelief in this rendition of 'For-e-ver Young'?

2

Sizakele to the Blood Ocean

Busisiwe Mahlangu

Gogo said that blood has its own life. She would hold my palm and cup it in both hands, trace the lines, and tell me that blood has its own journey. Looking at my palm, she told me things about my life. Gogo had bad eyes but she saw the future. She saw my mother's death first in the hair. It was not falling off but when she touched it she knew the worst was coming. I cannot imagine what that felt like, to have her heart broken twice, first by knowing and then understanding that there was nothing she could do about it.

She always told me stories, and now that the worst has come to pass, I know they were more than stories. She was handing something over, and in listening I did not realise what I was accepting. Somewhere in the folktales, Gogo was preparing me for this day. My favourite one was the story of the Blue Blood People, they also called themselves Moy'olwandle because they were born of the ocean and it was the ocean's breeze that blew them to the land. Gogo told this story like a chant. She never skipped a word or a sentence. She never started at the end or forgot to tell a part of it. Gogo told this story like a simple routine, the same way she told it the first time: clean, careful, and full of teeth.

"Sizakele," she would begin, "light the candle."

Then her voice morphed into the sound that pulls waves to shore.

This is how we would travel; with a match to the candle, with Gogo's voice filling the room eNdulwini. While the body remained grounded in Tembisa, my mind went wherever her voice led. My grandmother's voice knew many places and many people. The story of Moy'olwandle began at the shore. She told me to never forget this. I do not forget.

***

You do not want to find yourself in places where death reeks or in places that remind you of what death stole from you. That is why Gogo refused to go to Tembisa Hospital. And if you managed to persuade her to get her leg checked, she then refused to take her medication. When you tried to strategically sneak it into her food, she then refused to eat. There's was no winning with Gogo, she was set in her ways, and even after years of struggling with her leg, she was convinced that she knew the cure. That it would come and unfold to her as a dream and she would know the source of her wounds and how to heal them. She didn't believe that the doctors and nurses know what they are doing. At most, she believed that they needed help – her help. But with the wait her leg swelled up, becoming the weight pulling down on her faith.

I understand her hesitancy now. I know that when I was young, too young to start school but old enough to ask questions, she and my mother disappeared into the hospital one day, but only Gogo returned. The hospital stole her daughter. She told me the full story when I was older: about how they sat on the floor for hours, that none of the on-duty staff had taken not so much as a glance, that the nurses told mother she was being noisy when she screamed in agony, that it was not the illness that killed her but the lack of care. There's no humanity in hospitals. This is the one story she told with tears streaming down her face. It was tender and raw on her tongue, and her voice was as rough as if coal was burning in her throat.

I promised her that when I finish my degree in sales and marketing, I would get a job in an office and afford to cover all her needs, including healthcare that is rooted in humanity or ubuntu and everything else she wanted.

***

Moy'olwandle is a myth. That is what the people believe. It is important that they believe this. It is important that they forget, that they retell this as a story instead. Do you know what people do to something they deem powerful? They want to own it so that they can bend it, twist it, and turn it inside out until they can find a way to make it serve them. What is true power if you cannot bend it to your will? The hunger for power stripped wonder and beauty from this world. It is like being so fascinated with the flame that you reach out to touch it, to worship it? No, to blind it.

Moy'olwandle were hiding and camouflaging in crowds. They were in plain sight, watching people around them get sick but healing them in secret. With each treatment a risk, each treatment a gamble; a choice between mending and staying safe. What choice is there to make when your gift is to *look* and immediately see what ails a person?

Looking was seeing the body come to life so that the body itself tells you where it hurts. It's in the blood. Blood is the carrier of life, and all illness can be understood by listening to its flow. Moy'olwandle people can see the blood and find the source of the pain. Whatever ache or pain, they could heal it. But being a healer doesn't mean being able to stop death. Death is as natural as life and there's no way around it. People expect a lot from healers. They want miracles and when you cannot deliver, they want you to suffer as well.

***

The story that is not a story anymore went like this: the spirit of Moy'olwandle did not live in all the Blue Blood People. The spirit chooses and only when the possessor of the spirit dies can she suggest someone else to carry it. But this is only a suggestion, the spirit can still reject you. The ritual: you drink a drop of blood of the spirit's predecessor, you say a prayer, "la kufika khona amanzi kukhona ukuphila". You admit water is powerful, water gives life, water can save you. This is how I come to stand over Gogo, her body cold in an empty room. The leg has found a way to stop her heart, and drained her remaining hope, but left one wish known. Suddenly the house has aged with her. And now that she is gone, it is also touched by death.

I am aware of what I am meant to do. Yet, enraged, wondering if it is worth it. If we did not have to hide, the spirit wouldn't hide either, and we wouldn't forget who we are. Moy'olwandle. Gogo learned this sorcery through dreams in her old age and wept that she did had not known she had had the spirit all along. I think she died of heartbreak. A healer learning of her gifts, coming to terms with the years of burials, one child swallowed by the grave after another. Three children, with my mother at the end.

But now it has opened again. To be stripped of community in that way, to be stripped of your gifts in that manner, to receive everything back only to leave it behind a second later. That was heartbreak. I hold Gogo's hand, cupping it in both of mine. The knife is in my back pocket, I repeat *la kufika khona amanzi kukhona ukuphila*, readying myself for when the blood touches my tongue, unaware of the transition that will follow after. I have to do this quickly. I am alone, as I should be, though I wish there was someone else's voice encouraging me not to fear divinity. Outside, people are singing 'Thato ya hao' under the white and magenta tent. Gogo's body arrived hours ago. Tomorrow she will be planted back into the soil. Thato ya hao, may your will be done. God's will perhaps, but I am thinking about the will of humanity. I am thinking about duty, I am thinking about Gogo's wish. My mind is scattered across many thoughts but the time I have been holding Gogo's hand feels like years.

But then there is a knock. It does not pull me out of this dream that is not a dream. Quickly, I prick grandmother's finger. The person at ther door says something about the body and viewing it. I want to shout back that there is no body. That in this room is only me and my grandmother and candlelight. I can feel the weight of her stories, all coming alive. Which were true and which were told to put me to sleep? I can hear my cousins in the hall, moving up and down. Do they know that Gogo's tongue told heavy history and what we were receiving through listening? Do they know the mammoth task that I am to inherit?

There's no one to answer these questions. I am alone, as I should be.

3

Igazi Liyathetha

Vuyokazi Ngemntu

blood

/blʌd/
noun

noun: blood

1. the red liquid that circulates in the arteries and veins of humans and other vertebrate animals, carrying oxygen to and carbon dioxide from the tissues of the body.
"drops of blood"

2. violence involving bloodshed.

3. family background; descent or lineage.

INFORMAL•US
a fellow black person.

"Igazi liyathetha"
Igazi: blood
Thetha: a verb denoting the act of speech.
Also a directive to speak
Ergo, (Our) blood speaks!

Garrulous in its nature, our blood screams the injustices perpetrated against it/us historically. Spills these dark red secrets and stains history's luxurious white carpet. Strangles the falsehoods — *butter for fat* — with its putrid, malodorous combination of copper and rot and keeps its chokehold until the lie screams "I cannot breathe!"

Shortness of breath.
Restricted air supply to the lungs.
Mouth gulps compensatory breaths. Ineffectual. Dry, purplish lips. (History loves purple on black. ~~Sorry, deviating.~~ Incoherent thought detected. Delete!) Decreased oxygen supply to the brain. Dizziness. Deflated lungs.

Between my diaphragm and I (Footnote: "Umntu ngumntu ngabantu": Lena yintetha yakwa Xhosa egxininisa ukubaluleka kobudlelwane kwane mvisiswano phakathi kwaba(kwa)Ntu. Kukho ntetha imbi ethi 'Amathambo ayathungelana' nesiyakuyinika ingqwalasela kwixa elizayo – khumbula: besisathetha ngegazi, sisithi liyathetha. Ntonje ndiludidi lomntu oluthetha apha naphaya.) Sorry but not sorry: I'm not in the habit of translating my blood. But as I was saying, **'Andikwazi kuphefumla'** because between my diaphragm and I, you'd be greatly pained to establish who's the more depressed.

Translate police boot to perpetual subjugation. To exclusionary socio-economics. To the Group Areas Act and the politics of proxemics. To Vilakazi Street and tear gas at Enyobeni.

I can't breathe.

22 kids claimed by the latter incident, 29 claimed to have been claimed by the former. ~~Where am I going with this?~~ Blood flows to where it must and at times ~~that is down the gutter.~~ 'Ghetto' and 'gutter' mean the same thing, really. ~~'Ghetto' is synonym for 'township',~~ which, I posit, is synonym for 'human dumping site' or, should you wish to invest in a richer hyperbole, 'concentration camp'.

Stellies. I've spent the entire afternoon walking and sitting on the unmarked graves of *Evoke earlier-mentioned US INFORMAL denotative meaning of blood*, to no consequence (yet?).
Mental note:
Burn mayisake to cleanse room.

Carry root in pocket at all times to deflect the pull of residual matter … always assume the worst of this topography. This shit —sorry, substitute expletive with the noun 'stuff' — works, ask the dead kin that sublet your body!

~~The flow of this text is incoherent, I know. Has long since deviated from its course.~~ Freud permitting (not that I need the permission of yet another dead white man!) 'Deviation' sounds a lot like 'divination'.

Makhe sibhul' amathambo, siwave athini …
Amathambo: a Xhosa Collective noun for 'bones', themselves composed of calcium and phosphorus and containing a substance commonly known as marrow and rich in blood stem cells …

Divination as an invocation of DNA memory.

The bones say **"I can't breathe"** as articulately as a #BLM poster. Eric Garner in 2014 and a litany of other black, brutalised, dehumanised bodies since time immemorial.

It is good divination protocol to blow on the bones. Breathe (life) into them, as it were.

"Rise, my people, rise!" sounds like something from a 'negro spiritual' and we're not yet in the territory of is'thunywa, so ignore that in favour with "Phakama, Dlozi! Sivusel' Amakhos' amakhulu namabutho, khulumani makhehla. Phakamisan' izikhali zenu niqond' endabeni. Nina naningayesab' impi, vesane niqondane nezith' esweni. Maye, sivikeleni. Nithuleleni? Ake nikhulumeni!"

DNA memory activated.

Blood as signifier of kinship/allusion to descent/connection to ancestry.

Igazi liyathetha.

Lithi, "Mzukulu, you won't believe what happened to me!"

To which I cup my hands, clap them twice to produce a two-beat percussive cadence that denotes gratitude. "Thokoza, khehla." Be content in the knowledge that I, your great *apply decimal infinity* child, am listening.

Gogo, somewhat encouraged, unburdens her constricted chest. Her words cascade rapidly out of my own mouth.
"Igotheldupinsomekindofweirdpurgatoryandcantseemtobe-abletoprogressfromheresoimgonnaneedyoururgenthelp."
I'm out of breath by the end of the sentence. The average human being can only sustain one breath for 15 seconds. I learnt this in Drama School. Many would argue that not much is learnt there, since the nature of the work is actually called 'play' ... I digress.

Gogo is stuck in a yonder realm and needs help to transcend. Her eyes bulge out of her sockets and her mouth assumes the shape of an inverted horseshoe motif as she pleads with me.

This sounds too much like deja vu. I got a similar message from a nondescript piece of matter in my brain earlier. How best to explain this to Gogo? These seances seldom conform themselves to logic.

I could never stomach the smell of blood. Pretty much the equivalent of a punch to my gut. An assault on my olfactory senses. The red is so palpable, I can taste it. So much for that exclusively plant-based diet, huh! The congealed particles stuck between my teeth, I (not for the first time in other, variable scenarios of no consequence to this telling) swallow many difficult truths about my heredity. The dowry of dispossession. Loss calls for grief. She never fails to answer. The tears are not mine alone. A cleansing.

My grandmother, congealed in my head, can neither breathe nor move.

Her convulsions transpose themselves from her own centre to my shoulders. *Hlehla, mngoma.* Counter-rhythmic, sporadic eruptions of '*Heeeyi!*' the only languaging my regressive brain is restricted to, this is a state of emergency!

An exclamation of recurrent pain accompanied by migraines, abdominal cramps, short, shallow breathing, trance-induced delirium, dilated eyes, muscle spasms, (phantom?) arthralgia, fluctuating vocal placement, xenoglossy and lethargy a la Warsan Shire '*all the women in me are tired*'.

Congested township streets.
Congested township sewers in the self-same streets. See 'Poo-poo Protest', 4 December 2013 …

Socio-economics obstruct the progressive flow of black bodies up the ladder of access. Denied vehemently by the regional administration. Unlike the river in Egypt, shack dwellers are not moved by the crocodile tears of poverty porn voyeurs who caricaturise their plight.

insert middle finger icon

There are no kwashiorkor-bellied babies to smile for your pics while elegantly balancing lantern-eyed carrion flies on their parched lips. No gaunt limbs to wave at you, nor muddy, calloused feet to give chase as your shuttle leaves the airport after the trip beneath the surface of your 'design capital of the world' delusions.

10 minutes ago, my autonomy was still intact. That was before a droplet of my blood coagulated and strangled my brain. Consequently, grandmother mistakes my mind for her vaskom and can be seen, heard, felt (et cetera) leisurely washing her dirty laundry in my soul. ~~This makes no sense.~~ Where do I end and where does she begin? Ouroboros has no answers and concentrates on swallowing his tail instead. This is madness!

Interesting fact 1a: the Zulu word for a lunatic, 'uhlanya' is also used to refer to isangoma.

Isangoma discerns information through the use of divination, prophesy, clairaudience, clairvoyance, clairsentience and clair-cognizance.

I see voices and hear presences.

Interesting fact 1b: The isiXhosa word for madness is **ukuphambana**, which literally translates to the intersection or collusion of two (or multiple) realities. Viewed this way, madness is the result of one's psyche standing at the intersection of multiple concepts of reality.

Unseen does not mean untrue. I embrace the madness ...

Speaking of prophets and diviners: **Nontetha Nkwenkwe**, being one such, was a mother of ten, a number later halved by infant mortality. Relevance? *The remainder of her surviving children equals the number of my own biological offspring. DOB: 05-05-83.* Black woman diviner = **mad black woman.**

Nontetha was committed to a mental asylum on 6 December 1922.

See: Witchcraft Suppression Act of 1895 of the Cape Colony.

Ukuboshwa, despite literally translating to **the act of being tied (up)**, means **to get arrested.**

I tie my midsection with a ceremonial cloth to quell the convulsions. Ibidane ties a prophetess' midsection to galvanise and anchor her spirit when performing ceremonies in the sea, river or underneath a waterfall. Moving water is a good omen that speaks to progress.

Let us pray: May the blood flow with ease. Unobstructed, continuous flow. May the waters keep gushing. May you be immersed in abundance. May your cup overflow. May your spirit survive your flesh.

Nontetha died in police custody on the 20th of May 1935. The coroner's report listed liver and stomach cancer as the cause of death. *The coroner was not a black woman. Nobody was there to testify to having heard her utter the words, "I can't breathe!"* and her bones remain undiscovered to date.

Intwaso is an ancestral cry for vengeance, the indictment of colonialism and the need for restorative justice.

Our grandmothers
are moving.   Slowly,
          surely,
Singing church hymns to opiate their brains against the traumas their mouths relegated to their blood.

We flow with impunity because we don't walk alone.

Occasionally, I can't breathe. I imagine time to act like the veins in our heads in allowing the intergenerational passage of the trauma embedded in our blood. To this effect, writing remains the only effective purgative known to me. Like the steps of the provincial legislature building on that stinky December 2013 day, *I'm full of shit when I don't write.*

Abadala have cunningly embedded their armour under my fingers. A few dozen of their machetes rest awkwardly under my tongue.

This mouth belongs to no sailor, though. It was either the words continue to gnash away at my head or be allowed to hack their way through this diatribe until 4:29 AM, making me late for the meeting in my dreams.

~~I don't expect this to make sense, given my disloyalty to chronology~~. It took a lot of time to write this. Took my blood even more lifetimes.

Interesting fact 2: The isiXhosa word for breath, spirit and air is umoya.

The practice of channeling and summoning all that you are is known as **ukuphahla**.

Like most healers imbued with is'thunywa and the gift of inciting healing through sound (some call this prayer, go figure!), Nontetha wore white garments and a matching cape.

Side note: In my mind I travel back to that mental hospital in Beaufort West to deliver bales of cancer bush, mathunga, umhlabel' omhlophe and umdlavuza to reverse the ravages of sickness.

I imagine her saying something like "By the power vested in me by uMoya, I now declare you ..."

Insert own affirmations

Bloody hell! I dare to breathe.

Abazindla: The Prologue

Fezeka Mkhabela

The beat of the drum is how my people are remembered. Through the rhythms and the flow of life is how we cultivated the energy of surrender. Siyazindla, Amazindla, Abazindla – the ones who look inward. The great power lies with the one brave enough to search within. Blood, soul, and mind lie at the heart of Abazindla. We are the descendants of the great Zindla, a Sanusi, who gained a deep understanding of the design of the celestial human body. Some legends believe she sat with the Creator who gave her the coded secrets of celestial engineering. We are tall, magnificent, dark like the night, locs effervescent reaching the soles of our flat feet. We command the flow of our blood healing our wounds with the blink of an eye! We decode the cryptic messages of our bodies from the follicles through to the coil of a hair and outlive Gods beyond river time with the beat of our hearts. We were once a revered nation of people who ruled with wisdom and love.

Nations from all over Alkebulan travelled along a monstrous river known as uHlanga to seek our knowledge. Some even believed we carried the elixir of immortality. When they arrived at the tall iron gates of the village, they were welcomed by the thud of a wooden drum wrapped in animal skin and valiant soldiers seated on black stallions bearing sharp spears. The village rose around three glorious stone pyramids. Each with a gold-encrusted tip that carried enough energy to power each hut. Visitors believed it to be magic.

I am Ndawe, the one chosen to tell this story. I am the great granddaughter of Nomndayi, the crippled. Nomndayi was the daughter of King Malangeni and his second wife Siyeza. She was blind, stooped harshly, and had not been blessed with the gifts of Zindla. The once revered nation, renowned for leading with wisdom and love, had become arrogant and saw her as a curse. They banished her, unknowingly cursing themselves.

***

The day of the banishment was the coldest of that century. The sun rose in the east, as it always does, tenderly warmed the earth but a sharp winter breeze pierced from the heavens as if they were mourning. An aluminous fire blazed from within Inzalo Yelanga, a crescent-shaped moon cave carved of stone and nestled behind the sublime deep blue waterfalls of uHlanga. The waters along the cave are guarded by Mamlambo. Only the most formidable leaders of the tribe clans are permitted to enter the sacred grounds. Inside, the council sat pompously, awaiting the arrival of the King. The air was thin. The fires that kept the chamber warm roared on either side. Engraved on the cave walls was the ancient tale of the Creator and Zindla exchanging the cosmic blueprint of existence, now a fading ancestral memory. The regal leaders gathered, dressed in flamboyant garments patterned with geometrical shapes and rainbow-coloured beads decorating their soil complexion. Four powerful clans ruled Abazindla. The Msomi clan led by Vika, the Thembu clan led by Mfanekazi, the Qhawe clan led by Zikhona, and the Dlamini clan led by King Malangeni. Each century marks the birth of new clan leaders, who are born with an unhealing scar shaped like a crescent moon at the back of their necks, believed to be the touch of their ancestors.

Vika had a troubled look on his face. His dark brown eyes were gloomy, with his lips pressed together. The familiar sound of the waterfall drowned out his thoughts. His mind fluttered into a distant memory of the dazzling wedding of his younger sister Siyeza and King Malangeni. The celebration was a feast filled with only the finest meats, impeccably brewed millet beer, and fresh fruits. It was a joyous night that symbolised the union of family and the consolidation of power. The King's first wife had failed to produce an heir, so it was Siyeza's duty to bring forth a perfect child which the gods denied. Vika, a man of integrity, was conflicted. He was the King's advisor but also a brother and an uncle. Unease quietly ate away at his spirit. Could his family be the carriers of the curse? Mfanekazi sat across from him, her eyes piercing into his flesh. Suddenly, the moist air felt suffocating as the tension rose.

"Nc-nc-nc, Vika kaMsomi, if you intend to defend your crippled niece today, be warned that my clan is prepared to stand behind me," barked the imperious Mfanekazi, pulling him abruptly from his sea of thoughts. Mfanekazi was a beautiful woman adorned in a magnificent cowrie shell headpiece. She was full of pride, with the taste of evil on her tongue.

"Commit treason, Mfanekazi, but do not use an innocent child as your pathetic excuse," challenged Zikhona, the loyal warrior who commanded the village military. He was the biggest, tallest and most menacing of the leaders. The tension thickened with the arrival of the King. The council rose in his presence but Mfanekazi maintained a sour disdain. Vika's eyes met Zikhona to thank him, but the commander remained uninterested.

"Nkosi yamakhosi," the council sang in unison. Malangeni wore a long leopard-skin cloak. He had high cheekbones, a sharp nose, and anguish in his eyes. He sank onto his throne, with the tumbling waters behind him.

"I have heard the cries of this council and the tribe. In the hundred thousand years of our tribe's existence, an impaired child has never lived among us. I have asked myself if we have angered the ancestors," he said as the council listened intently.

Mfanekazi stood, "King, the more this cripple you call your

daughter remains within this tribe, the greater *isinyama* it brings. We are the living gods of this land; what will our enemies think of us when they cast eyes on that horror–"

Vika screamed, "I will kill you with my bare hands if you continue to speak of her in that way!"

Mfanekazi smirked, quite pleased with herself. Malangeni commanded silence in the cave. The pitter-patter of the waterfall filled the air. He motioned for Mfanekazi to sit down. She grudgingly obeyed. Malangeni carried a deep love for his daughter despite being ashamed of her. For close to a decade councils sat before him, persuading him to cast out the curse before it's too late! Vika had supported him all these years but even their alliance was not strong enough to prevent a rebellion.

"Mother of the Thembu clan, you will watch how you speak or leave my council." Malangeni took a deep breath and hung his head in shame, preparing to do the unthinkable.

Long before a messenger whispered in her ears, Nomndayi already knew. The cold walls of her rondavel swallowed her whole as she sat on her reed mat for the last time in the village of her ancestors. She accepted her fate because her father had forsaken her. She felt rejected, discarded, and worthless. Her happiest memory of her life had been in her mother's womb. There she had been at peace and protected.

***

My great grandmother spent her exile deep in the frosted mountains of Gazi Elimhlophe where Vika raised her as his daughter. Each day at dusk she played the rhythm of her heartbeat on her drum. However, on the eve of her nineteenth birthday, something unexpected had happened. As the pulse of the beat began, a blue electromagnetic current as pale as her faded eyes began to illuminate in spirals around her thick brown locs. An ancient code was weaving into her hair, marking the first time she received a message beyond death and time.

I inherited her power and it is my duty to deliver these sacred messages to the very people who exiled the mother of my mothers. The blood that courses through her veins is the same blood that gives me life. When I look within, I feel the rushing of its streams like the oceans crashing into the forbidden rivers of old. Zindla, our great ancestor, has chosen me as she chose Nomndayi.

5

Umcimbi Wegazi

Luyolo Vukuza

Kungaqhawuk' ibhobhile kuphele uyolo kubathungi. Lento iyingulo inawo amandla okuliqweqwedisa ixhoba lide libesisigculelo sentlebendwane, nempatheko mbi yabo basazibona beyimiqabaqaba. Ngamanye amaxesha ukugula kusuka kubengumdaniso wamasele, into enolawulo ol.uhesheheshe nolungena kuthintelwa ngowegazi nenyama, kude kusungule nomphefumlo wexhoba kushiye umzila womzimba othwele ukufa.

Kwisithili saseNtabankulu, phesheya kwelali zakwaBhaca phonoshono nomlambo iBhuwa, eNtilini yafumaneka idayimane eluthuthwini iqaqambile ingabonwa 'mntu, inyibib'ityatyambo evelele eziny'ityatyambo ngokuqaqamba intombi kaNomsa Mzumbe, uZanyiwe Mzumbe. Ukuzalwa kukaZanyiwe emva kweminyaka uNomsa ephuncukelwa kwaza noxolo olukhulu kusapho luphela. Kumhla lathi tha ilanga ukuvela kwalomafungwashe emva kwenzame ezininzi. Wakhula ke ngenene umntwana de wafikelela kwisigaba sokuba aqale isikolo. Uwachuchile ke amabanga wakhe kungeko ntetho imbi ngaphandle kwezo ezazisuka kootitshala, oontangandini nabazali bakhe, xa bemncoma ukuba yingqondi nanje ngoko wayetshotshele kwizifundo zakhe, kungekho esimongameleyo. Kwalile xa engena esinaleni kwangathi obu bukrelekrele bakhe busuke babhanguza amadangatya ngoku, batsho ngesibani esathi sayikhanyisa yonke loo lali yaseNtilini. Abafuna ukubhalela izizalwane zabo, abafuna ukubhalelwa ileta zaseburhulumenteni nee-obhitshwari, babesiza kulenzwakazi ifike ibaqhawule ngobubele. Ufunde ke umntwana wade waya kuthi gxada, kwibanga le shumi elinesibini. Kulapho ke unina ekhabe ngawo omane wathi, "unotshe owam umntwana ahlale nje kulonyaka ozayo, ngesizathu sokuba ndiyimpula kalujaca ndixolele ukumis'amabele, ndifunga uyise elele kobandayo."

Ngenene wawaqokelela amasentana uNomsa evuka ngonyezi ethwalela abantu iinyanda, esenza ivasi zakwamlungu aphinde amane ebamba nasemasimini. Uthe uphela ke unyaka wabe sele ekhathule noko, kubonakala ngenene ukuba akalali umfazi ozeleyo. Kaloku wayexolela ukudinwa abeyimfe kunokuba usana lwakhe lufane naye, libe liqabakazi elichutywe lalahlwa ziinzingo neemeko zedlakadlaka lendlala. Wayethe katya ukuyithanda intombi yakhe nokuba wawungeke umve esitsho, yona imisebenzi yakhe neendlela awayemxhasa ngayo yayizixela. Wawungafunga umunc'intupha uthi lo mfazi akazange amelamanise uZanyiwe, kodwa inyaniso yeyokuba babekho oXolile, Sindiswa kunye noXoxo abathi bavela emva kokuba kuzelwe lembelukazi imanzandonga ingu Zanyiwe.

"Uthi ufundela ukuba yintoni na Zen?" lavakala lisitsho ngolunye urhatya ixhegokazi liqongqotha umbheka phesheya walo litshaya. "Ndifuna ukuba ngutitshalakazi mama, andiziboni ndisenza msebenzi wumbi ngaphandle kokuhlohla inzala yamaAfrika" waba nolunda unina akuyiva lempendulo, wayebhongoza de kubengathi uyadlisela kwabanye abafazi enelizwi elalisithi, "ukuzala kukuzolula" xa eyisongayo intetho yakhe, iyinto eyayisele ithande ukudala umdintsi nomona ekuhlaleni.

Ngenene kanye xa kuvulelwa unyaka olandelayo yagaleleka incwadi esuka kwaNokholeji (eFort Hare) ixela ukuba uZanyiwe uyamkelwa kwisicelo sakhe sokuqeqeshelwa ubutitshala, ufundele ke kuleDyunivesithi yaseAlice. Wawelwa ngumqa esandleni wokufumana isikolo kanye kulelali akhulele kuyo. Uhlohlile ke eBhuwa Senior Secondary School, ethe rhatya ukuba nothando nobubele ntoleyo eyamenza ukuba afumane inyweba yokubekwa njengesandla senqununu. Isitsho samaXhosa sithi, ingcwaba lentombi lisemzini. Nyani ke uye wazimanya ngeqhina lomtshato nomfana wakwaNdlovu abathi balizwa ngabantwana abane ababetsho ngolusu olumthubi buntsundu ingathi bobo bukanina. Lomfo wakwaNdlovu ke akazange abenalo ithamsanqa kuba kaloku uThixo wakhawuleza wayisonga iminyaka yakhe kwelihlabathi wandwendwela kweloyisemkhulu umfan'esaze ngobuso ezweni. Wathi wawelwa ngumgodi eRhawutini nanje ngoko wayeyibhasibhoyi khona.

Esi ke yabasisiqalo sokucinezeleka nokuxhwaleka kwalom-tshakazi ethukwa kushiywe elilityelweyo ngabasemzini. Wona amadodakazi sele ekhwela ezehlela emana ukuthi "ewe kaloku ubulele ubhuti kuba ebuza uyise walemigqakhwe." Kulapho ke uNomsa esukume waya kulanda intombi yakhe eyiboleka ngelithi usafuna ikhe iyombophela inyanda uyafa yiqabaka, ezibika nokukhumbula abazukulu bakhe. Likhathule ixesha kungekho mntu obuza omnye nomtshakazi wabonisa ukuxola nasemsebenzini wabuyela wayimbokodo, waqaqamba nje ngesiqhelo. Kwalile ngaminazana ithile wazibika intloko emana imthi nqaku iphinde inyamalale. Iye ikhula ngokukhula lengulo kwabonakala ukuba ithande ukuxaka de isikolo samkhulula ukuba akhe ayophumla abuye xa sele engcambaza. Isuke yaqina ngokuqina intloko, emana ukumongoza ngamanye amaxesha. Unina wayewa evuka ehamba oosiyazi nezibhedlela, emana ukucela kulento yabantwana xa eyibona intombi yakhe iphelela kumandlalo oku kwebhedi kamahlalela.

Zona iintlungu zazisele zilinkankathe kanobom ixhoba. Oosiyazi noogqirha basemlungwini babesele bencazelana ngayo le bhekile ingundabamlonyeni, intlungu yakhe iyinto yokucela ikofu kwezondibano zabo belilisela ngelinye elithi yingqumbo yeminyanya, sisibetho sokhokho kusini na? Abantu belali babemana ukunqwala iintloko bakulibona ixhoba limcingana okwabafazana bewela umlambo. Lalisele liyinkomo endla yodwa, izihlobo nabasemzini behle ngomcinga, unina nesizukulu sakhe babetshintshana ngayo lentlungu yeligqiyazana eyayingatyiwa

nayinja. Laliphila nje ngomoya, wona umzimba uthwel'ukufa.
Kaloku kwakungekho nto yayingazanywanga, izibhedlele,
amagqirha nabathandazeli kodwa babuye nembande yesikhova.
Le ntsumantsumane yalibetha lazizicuku usapho lwakwaMbovu,
elowo nalowo esithi uhamba nini usihlekisa ngabantu nje.
Maxa wambi kwakuye kubenzima xa usapho lusolwa ngobugqi
obuthethwa yintombi yalo. Kaloku ingulo yayisele imana
ukumenza angene emizini athethe izinto ngabantu balapho
abangasekhoyo, womva esithi ubalekile uzibani ngetshe,' nto leyo
eyayibenza abahlali bafutheke ngumsindo bafune ukulitshisa
liphila ixhoba.

Into yayingumnqa kulengulo, maxa wambi wayelibona izulu
lingekahlomi nokuhloma abe sele elichaza ukuba lizakuna.
Uke wathi ngenyimini kusemtshatweni wavakala esithi
"Ndibona ilifu elimnyama kwesi siqalo lizakuthela. Ndibona
xhewukazi liwel'umlanjana lijonge apho kufele khona ithole, 'lithi
lomfazana makakhulule imbadada lomhlaba azonyathela kuwo
ungcwele.' Wafutheka wayimfe umtshakazi akuziva ezindaba
eme ngelithi tata kaEnzo, khupha lomthakathi wephambana
apha uzokundonela usuku. Kungentsuku zatywala kwavakala
ukuba umtshakazi ulala notatazala wakhe yaye, indlalifa lena
kamakoti, ngumninawa womyeni wakhe. Yonke lengcumbembe
yathi yavakala akube ezixhomile umtshakazi. Baqala abantu
bathi makube unentloko emhlophe kuba kaloku nanko ebona
izinto ezisazokwenzeka lento yakhe ifuna nje umntu ephehlweni
bangqina batsho abantu, labe lisamile icala elithi yintakatho le qha
qwaba! Inguloqulukubhode wezimvo.

Kuthe ngaminazana ithile kanye xa lithambekayo ilanga, yavuka
intokazi enkulu igquma ngathi inamadimoni, koko ingabikwa
hlaba, isukume kumadlalwana wayo yazulazula apha endlwini
phofu kungekho lizwi ilenzayo. Imane ithetha yodwa, kodwa
kwezozisebesebezo kungekho nto ephumayo nenambithekayo.
Kwakulentetho inye wawuyakumva ehleka, ebonakalisa umsindo,
uphinde umve engxengxeza. Ibeyilompithizelo bexakiwe aba-
ntwana endlwini kungekho othethayo. Kwakweso sithuba kanye
angene ngaso uNomsa endlini, naye wafika wama nematha

akubona lomnqa. Kuthe kusenjalo kusuke kwabonwa ngomntu emana ukungqubeka eludongeni, ephuthaphutha eludongeni. Yamothusa kakhulu uNomsa lento de wathumela umzukulwana wakhe ebumelwaneni ukuba makaphuthunywe ngesitaliyoni okanye iguruguru ufuna ukuleqisa intombi yakhe kwagqirha, ayimnandanga mpela ngoku. Ufike esibhedlela iSpetu Hospital yajongwa yajongwa le meko, ugqirha waphuma nelithi mayisiwe kwisibhedlela sabagula ngengqondo kuba zonke ezimpawu zintama ukuba kutenelwe endlini. "Intombi le ifuna ukusiwa koogqirha bengqondo nanje ngomntu obeke waphangela esikolweni inokuba ingqondo yakhe ikhathele ifuna uhoyo labaxilonga iingqondo" yatsho ingxelo kagqirha.

Ekuhambeni kwexesha waqala wabonisa nezinye iimpawu ezifana nokwehla komzimba, ukuxhuzula, iingxaki zamehlo njalonjalo, nto leyo emtsho kwanzima nokuhamba egevuzela namadolo. Kuthe kungantsuku zatywala wabe sele eligoqololo leyosiyosi elingakwazi nokuya endlwini encinci, engulomntu ogugela kumandlalo. Mhla latshon'emin'ilanga kwaMzumbe, kusibekele engqondweni, bathe besekulontlungu gqi isipheke-pheke senkwenkwana iphethe imvulophu emdaka ngebala eyayineleta eyayimema umzali wesiguli nesiguli ukuba maba-ncede bafike esibhedlela kwangentseni yangolwesine.

Bathe bakusibona abantu belali sichulukunyathela ucwambu isiguli sakwaMzumbe sele singangenaliti bamana ukujongana, de wavakala omnye esithi le ntombazana inezigulo zabantu abatsha, abanye yaba ngumcimbi ekumele wenziwe, abanye beza nezabo iintlebo.

Bafike esibhedlela, bathi folokohlo kulomngcelele wawusele uphuphuma okweTinarha kakade. Ngecala emva kwentsimbi yethoba wagaleleka ugqirha wayalela ukuba acelele usapho lakwaMzumbe uzakuqala ngalo ukuxelenga. "Mama uMzumbe nawe Mrs. Ndlovu, mandiqale ngokunamnkela ndikwanibulisa ngalentsasa. Ndicela ukuphinde ndibulele ukuba niphuthume nazo kusabela ubizo xa nicelwayo nokuba isicelo ndisenze sele kuhlwile. Into endinibizele yona namhlanje yeyokuba sikhe sathetha nogqirha uJame Blemdaw waseJamani nongumpond-zihlanjiwe kwelengqondo icandelo. Kulapho ke ethe wajonga ifiles zikaMrs Dlomo waphinda wacela imifanekiso bhanyAbhanya yeMRI scanner.

Uke wathi cwaka umntu omkhulu emva kwalamazwi, wa-khokha umoya, wandula ukugqibezela intetho yakhe "Ndiyicelele uxolo indawana yokuba siyibona sele kuhlwile lengozi, engqon-dweni kaMrs Ndlovu sifumane amahlwili nangunobangela wayo yonke lengulo. Kuthiwa ke xa ibizwa yi BRAIN ANEURYSM. Kuphinde kubekho nentsolo zokuba nako ukuba ngumhlolokazi kumkhathazile uMrs Ndlovu de kwadala uxinzelelo lwengqondo." wachaza de wafikela kwinto yokuba sele kungasekho kubuyela mva nakulithintela ihlwili, sele lilikhulu kakhulu.

Kungentsuku zatywala uZanyiwe waqalwa kukungasebenzi kwemilenze yakhe de kwabe nomzimba uyachaphazeleka. Kwalile ngenye imini wavuka ejijeke nomlomo lo ujonge ecaleni, engakwazi nokuthetha. Wawungaphika ukuba sesiya siqumama sentombi kaNomsa xa umbona. Kodwa kuthe ngentsasa elandelayo kwavukwa ethembisa, noninzi lwamalungu omzimba ekwazi ukuwasebenzisa. Nokuba wayengakwazi kuhamba nje kodwa uncumo lwalubhalwe ebusweni neendaba ekwazi ukuzitsho ngathi uzifunda ephepheni, kanti uyabakhohlisa. Wasuka wangathi uya-khohlela suka watsala umxhelo wabe uyalishiya eli limagade ahlabayo. Kwavakala ngesikhalo esikrakra ukuwa komthi omkhulu, ushiya kusezintsizini, kumnyama entla.

"Ushiya umzila nelahleko enkulu, ishiya nemibuzo ethi kazi liyakutshona kuthethwa eyiphi xa likwazile ukusiphula umthi omkhulu kangaka. Liwugawule ngokungena lusizi namfesana siii! UMCIMBI WEGAZI, awunagqirha, awunamboni ungena uncumile ushiye isingqala. Ithemba linye lisekuxhasaneni nokuthandana, kuba lento iyingulo lutshaba lwayo nayiphi na into ephila phantsi kwelanga, yaye akuzi ngazingqi. Kazi lonyaka liwile nje igorhakazi ngubani ozophinde ancancis'ezintsana? Siii! kufa ulixelegu" latsho elinye lamaxhego lakuwuva umphanga wokusweleka kuka-titshalakazi. Eneneni isitya esihle asidleli. Ntinga ntaka ndini ngoku usenako, lento ilixesha ayicengi ndolala phi.

6

The Form of the Fibre
is Shaped by the Follicle

Jarred Thompson

Barber

I've been cutting his hair since he came home from the hospital so I know that when he shakes, there's a tic on the way.

I trust you. He holds his neck. The shaver buzzes through his crimp.

You've got all kinds of curl, I say. (Like the neurons in your head.)

No! He shakes. Yells.

I stop. Mr Tourrettes has his own ideas and wants to be heard.

Fuck shit bitch whore fuck shit bitch whore.

I tell him the relaxer is going to break the bonds, that we can't do this often because every follicle has a clock and you don't wanna fast forward into a bald scalp now, do you?

Deadest dead deadest deader dead … he bounces up and down.

I rearrange his hair. Make it point true north. Straight. *It doesn't do anything,* he points. Hair webs around our feet.

Later, sweeping the curls into the bin, I finger the bald spot behind my earlobe and dab Amla oil on it with my pinkie.

Apartment

The Harry Potter bobblehead stares at the bulb-less tree stump of a lamp. The TV: an opaque window. The radio: a static mist. Outside: cold.

She has taught him how to moisturise from the root. Start at the tip, comb down to the follicle, and stretch a decade into a grip (it slips between his fingers).

They take turns doing each other, sitting in between legs. The room is hotter than it's meant to be, thanks to the coals at their feet.

"Do you remember that time a woman found God in the veins of a tomato?" He wraps her hair around curling rods.

She likes the pull on her sculpt, the slight jolt running down her spine. "Yeah, they even consulted a food science department to preserve it."

Silence retains its shape, no matter what they say. Death lies on the windowsill outside, but at least they have this.

"Maybe it won't be so bad. Pushing reset, going back to scales—" He stops, surveys his handiwork.

"—crawling back into the ocean, amphibians refusing their legs." Her head drops.

For a moment he thinks she's breaking down.

"It feels so good. The pulling—" She doesn't finish her sentence, feels for her hair and laughs. "You're having fun making tornadoes, huh?"

Outside, water wrinkles the city into marsh.

Burial

The body is brought down through the narrow passage, pulled from the crawl space and negotiated through fissure, furthest from the cave mouth. It takes a day to get there, but they are two. One cradles the head, another cups the feet, and the *drip-drip-drip* on their shoulders.

They've trekked this passage before. When the light gives out they know to feel around for the hole beyond the archive of stalagmites, in the bedding plane of limestone.

Arrived, they nestle mother between kin and smear olive oil on her hardening skin. Her limbs swirl inward, toward her belly, the way a centipede might contract when touched by the tip of something it doesn't understand.

They sigh. Sound fills the throat, echoing in chambers above them. The sigh is a word they've made together. A word only spoken here. The word is their name for this death that life keeps packing together and forcing out of its follicle.

They go to work removing mother's hair with the jagged end of stone cores. Hair is the last tether. Then, they beat their fists against a crack in a column. The cavern rubbles, slightly.

When they surface it is night. A fire is made. A pelt of hair is laid as a pillow. By morning, the dew has turned the pillow into a bowl. Constellations of berries lie in the mud. This is breakfast.

A camphor tree thaws in the sun and gives up its scent. The scent whistles in the nostril; the smell a prayer spoken with the palms. Another fire is made. The hair is drowned in it.

They eat by its heat.

7

Fix the Hair, Fix the Child

Sithembiso Khalishwayo

Dear Sir,

I have come across some valuable information that might assist in my next article. I know that it might be disquieting to some, but it is a story that needs to be shared. This involves the work currently underway at the Institute of Rebirth and the rumours of children who might not have the same hair as us. I do hope that we are able to publish this story. If not, I will tender my resignation by the end of this month.

Sincerely,
Andrew Worethone

Annual Report

by Dr DeVa LaMa

Khumbulani has gone through all the motions of an abandoned child, going from one foster home to another. The Institute has had many subjects like him with minimal success. Most of them have either gone missing or have broken away from the programme which has affected our study and the Institution's bottom line. We were aiming for an 80%

success rate for them to be reintroduced into society. The team and I have been working with four subjects that I am confident will make for the perfect study as the subjects should balance each other out.

Khumbulani's gullibility and his insecurities could be used to our advantage through emotional manipulation. His hair shaft abnormalities, which have caused brittle, short, and unruly hair, is to be corrected through targeted treatment. There is a hope to introduce him back into our society as an average looking, functioning child, into the care of a suitable family which may diminish the frequency of his instability and depression, limiting his independence and ambition.

Sashi, our first subject, showed great promise in the original trials for Hirsutism, using the Sudipel treatment. In phase two clinical trials, we observed the possibility of future infertility due to her condition, this is of grave concern. We have decided to increase her fertility drug intake sooner rather than later, with the goal of increasing her chances of producing offspring, preferably female, when she comes of age. This would enable us to continue to harvest the stems cells and DNA of her descendants to further our research and to maintain a steady birth rate in our society. Her intelligence, leadership capabilities and carefree attitude will need to be kept in check if she is to become the model of an obedient wife and mother.

Ember has been a problematic child since her introduction to the trials. By deciding against returning Ember to The Farm for reevaluation of the underlying complexities of her condition, the Board of Directors dismissed my recommendation offhand.

We cannot treat what we do not understand. Her curly hair does not conform to our vision and mission of the norms we would like to encourage in our society. It is complicating our research as it renders her disposition less pliable to social coercion. For this to work, she cannot be on her own. Being among others will compel her to seek stability and lead to her tackling her tendency towards rage. This is not passion or focus as she claims it is. Her failure to fall in line could *jeopardise the programme and threaten the achievement of the goals we have for our society.*

Abungu has been a very interesting and challenging case in the months we have had him under observation, due to his extreme case of Alopecia Areata. Due to the sensitivity of the subject of his family's legacy, which may in future affect the political landscape of our society, a small group of highly capable scientists are working on his condition. We have isolated Abungu to West Wing for his own safety and have limited his interactions with other children to Sashi, Khumbulani and Ember (whom may yet turn to our way of thinking). This inner circle of influence and loyalty could aid in his expectations of leading the people of our society. First, he needs to look the part. We are struggling with moderating his overly cautious and stubborn demeanour. We need to harvest more suitable hair from THE FARM immediately. This is priority number one.

Diary Entries

Khumbulani: I was promised a better tomorrow. That I would be safe. That I could be cured. They told me that they had found the family I needed, the family that would love me forever. They came to my home, in one of those minibuses. There was a man in a white suit who gave my parents, my foster parents, some kind of envelope. As I waved them goodbye from the back of the minibus, the last thing I remember my parents telling me was to write them. I wasn't alone in the minibus. There were about 10 or 12 children in there. Their hair looked very strange, others' just like mine. We drove for a very long time. The man in the white suit gave me something to drink, I don't remember much about the ride after that. What I do remember is stopping at a farm that read IOR FARM, but there weren't any animals that I could see. All the children got off, except for me. There was a girl just behind the minibus. She stood there and stared at me through the back window as the distance between our faces widened. The puzzled look on her face mirrored my own confusion.

The minibus rolled away before I could form a complete thought and mouth "Where are we? What's going on? I don't remember her in the minibus, but I waved her goodbye.

Sashi: It all started on that day, my big celebration. The day I finally got accepted for treatment of my condition. I worked hard and dedicated myself to ensuring my selection in the first group trial. I had big dreams, with the help of Institute of Rebirth I've always been somewhat more determined than most of the children I grew up with, and revelled in goal-setting and planning from a young age. Mom gifted me with my first ever 'Goals' notebook for my sixth birthday. I kept one from that year on. I carried the book wherever I went. I could be the best version of myself without any judgement. The future looked bright, thanks to the Institute of Rebirth. I stepped outside with my mom holding my one hand, my book in the other. My dad was at work that day. A man in a white suit greeted us, gave mom an envelope and walked me to his car holding the door open to let me in. I felt special. This was my moment, my day of acceptance.

Ember: It was just another day at that school. Same old bullying, for not looking like them, performing like them. Each time, each fight, I was the problem. The teachers treated me differently to all the other children. They wanted to change who I was. I resisted. They were relentless. I felt a sudden, firm tug on my hair as soon as I reached for the door handle of the Beetle when my mom came to pick me up after school. Until then, my father seemed to pass peacefully. Instead of heading home to breathe a sigh of relief after a long day of holding my breath, awaiting a new blow, this man in a white suit was dragging me by the hair and this man in a white suit threw me into the boot of a minibus. My mother didn't say or do anything, she just looked on as if I wasn't her daughter. As if she was one of them.

For a while afterwards I could hear nothing but the ceiling-to-floor carpet muffled sound of the vehicle gliding across the tarmac. The vehicle guiding me to God knows where and my body conducting the vibrating thrum of its animating diesel engine, my back against the walls of this mindless machine. The minibus would keep on moving and stopping. With each stop, I could hear the voices of other children growing louder. The minibus finally made a complete stop, the voices of the other children started to fade away until all I could hear was the click of the boot opening. The sun's rays hurt my eyes as they pulled me out the boot. I could barely see the outlines of the other children standing in front of me. As the minibus rolled away, I saw a shadowy figure of a boy or a girl looking out the back window waving at me. Why were they still in the minibus? Where were they going while we were left there, in front of this farm? I didn't recognise any of the children there, not from anywhere. It didn't take long to realise, we were different, we were the rejects. We were never welcomed in our homes so they sent us here.

Abungu: They took me away from him, my teacher, my best friend, my father. Life in the lake house was all I had ever known. My father always assured me that I was meant for something great, that they could fix me, that one day I would lead the people, the society, to a glorious future. Where we could all be the same. On that day, we flew over the great city, and signalling down with his long fingers spread out to the clusters of concrete-grey and ice-blue skyscrapers reaching up to the skies, he said that one day it would all be mine. That people down there would always look up to me even when I'm gone. We flew over a farm and landed on a tall building called the Institute of Rebirth. That was the first time I met Dr DeVa LaMa. The first time I came upon a person outside the lakehouse. The first time I met the man in the white suit. He called me Sir. My father gave him an envelope. The man smiled at my father, my father got back into the helicopter and left. That was my first time without my father by my side. The journey to fix me had begun.

The Trial

Judge Hillary: It has come to my attention that you have not reached the eighty per cent positive outcome that you promised the Institute. How did you allow these four children to escape and change the course of our work that our society has been doing for the past five centuries, Doctor?

Dr DeVa LaMa: I do apologise your Honour. It appears that their hair has somehow enabled them to rebel against the systems I put in place.

Judge Hillary: Will you be able to find them before things fall apart? Before they find the other children we have lost?

Dr DeVa LaMa: Yes, your Honour. I just need more time. The Institute won't let you down. I won't let you down again.

Judge Hillary: This is the last time I want to see you in this court room. Fix the hair …

Dr DeVa LaMa: Fix the child

***

Dear Sir,

I haven't received any feedback for my proposed article, I would like to know why your response is being delayed.

Sincerely,
Andrew Worethone

***

Dear Judge Hillary and Dr DeVa LaMa,

One of my young reporters is in the process of exposing the Institution and its operations. We need to find those four children before their escape poses a greater threat to the survival of the society and our way of life.

Fix the hair, fix the child.

Sincerely,
James Johnson

***

Do you think we'll ever find others like us?

The world won't take us back, so we have to. We have to.

BLOOD/BRAIN/BARRIER:
A Mindplay

by Nicole Thackwray

1. INT. LATE BUS - NIGHT

OTIS (26) rubs divots into his temples. Pale,
sweat-slick, he nearly comes unhinged with every
jolt of the bus under him.

In a pilling sweater - big square glasses, forearms blooming yellow-black with bruises - he
conjures images of damp apartment walls, gro-
cery-store cologne, or forgotten laundry.

The shuttle is largely empty. Falling apart in
the way that only government-buses can: loose
panels and seats exposing their foam. NURSES and
SECURITY GUARDS turn their faces from the interi-
or, towards the rhythm of the streetlamps.

                    BUS RADIO
          (jangly, humming)
          ... When you think the night
          has seen your mind, that
          inside you're twisted and
          unkind ...

Otis presses his tongue to his soft-palate, grimaces. Blood slicks his gums like ruddy diesel.

CUT TO

2. INT. DOCTOR'S OFFICE - EARLY EVENING -
   FLASHBACK

The DOCTOR is a jowly middle-aged man who wears
his exhaustion in deep creases. His authoritative
knuckle raps at a scan of Otis's brain. An inky
road-system of veins, fractal upon fractal of
y-splits, is circled in dry-erase marker.

IRIS IN

In the gyre - a dark mass.

                    DOCTOR
          (voice shifting in and out of
          focus through Otis's throbbing
          headache)
          ... Haemophiliac ... Highly
          unusual ... Low blood flow ...
          Otis? ... AneurysmAneurysmAn-
          eurysm--

3. INT. LATE-SHIFT BUS - BACK TO THE PRESENT

The bus halts, impatiently, at a stop street. Just
ahead, a broken down hatchback. A young couple
spills from its doors, gesturing, panicky, neither
able to figure out how to open the bonnet. White
engine-smoke dissipates into the foggy evening.

The bus driver sighs deeply, taps at the gear-
shift with his index finger. The pressure builds -
that simple notion of fluid dynamics. In blood, as
in traffic, we cannot see force - only how things
respond.

                    BUS RADIO
          ...Let me stand to show that
          you are blind. Please put
          down your hands, 'cause I see
          you...

4. INT. DOCTOR'S OFFICE - EARLY EVENING -
   FLASHBACK

The doctor taps away at an old keyboard, filling
out a virtual prescription. He exhales, rolls his
chair back, and faces Otis.

                    DOCTOR
          Our treatment options are limit-
          ed. I've written up something to
          lower your blood pressure, but
          we'll have to monitor it care-
          fully.

5. INT. LATE-SHIFT BUS - BACK TO THE PRESENT

Otis winces, pushing the sides of his head together as if to keep them from splitting.

                    ANEURYSM
          Hear that? You could have a
          parasocial relationship with
          your aneurysm!
          (beat)
          Doesn't get more "careful mon-
          itoring" than that.
          (beat)
          Come on, buddy, it's me!

                    OTIS
          Shut up. Shut the fuck up.
          You're not real, you're just
          blood--

                    ANEURYSM
          You love blood! That's what
          that means. Haemo, for blood,
          philia, for looove...

Otis's breath quickens. He forgets that this conversation, much like his aneurysm, is only going
on inside his head.

                       OTIS
          (panicky, loud)
          My blood doesn't clot,
          asshole! It's a death sentence.

The other passengers stir from their disinterest,
look over at Otis with irritation, perhaps
concern.

The conversation returns to the brain.

                    ANEURYSM
          Life sentence, death sentence,
          same thing. And your blood did
          clot, so there.

                       OTIS
          I hate you.

                    ANEURYSM
          You don't hate me. I am you.

                       OTIS
          No, you're not. You're just a
          stupid clump of cells.

                    ANEURYSM
          Hey, I'm only here because
          your blood still has protec-
          tive instincts.

                         OTIS
          Right, deadly papercuts and a
          clot in my brain.

                       ANEURYSM
          And you got to meet me!

                         OTIS
          I haven't met you. You're not real.

                       ANEURYSM
          Oh, I'm real alright. A doctor
          wouldn't entertain a delusion,
          would he?

6. INT. DOCTOR'S OFFICE - EARLY EVENING -
   FLASHBACK

The doctor shifts in his chair, an uneasy look
comes over him. Otis stares off into the middle
distance.

                        DOCTOR
          Otis, are you with me? I need
          you to understand the serious-
          ness of--

Otis is somewhere else.

7. INT. LATE-SHIFT BUS - BACK TO THE PRESENT

                         OTIS
          (quietly)
          So, what are you, anyways?

                       ANEURYSM
          Just a couple of proteins
          coming together, the most
          natural thing in the world.

Otis sighs, leans into the condensation-covered
bus window, grateful for the cold.

                    OTIS
          Like talking to an aneurysm.

                  ANEURYSM
          I'm two planets eclipsing.
          A tiny ballsack in your skull.
          Look at me, I'm right here.

Otis's eyes roll back into his head, a scrolling
texthead prints across his inner eyelids. Otis
sighs, presses his thumbs into the crests of his
eye sockets.

                  ANEURYSM

```
mmmmmmmmmmmmmmmmmmmmmmmmmmmmmmmmmmmmmmmmmmmmmmmmmm
mmmmmmmmmm^^^^^^mmmmmmmmmmmmmmmmmmmmmmmmmmmmmmmm
mmmmmmmmm/        \mmmmmmmmmmmmmmmmmmmmmmmmmmmmmm
mmmmmmmm/   @   @   \mmmmmmmmmmmmmmmmmmmmmmmmmmmm
mmmmmmm/      0      \mmmmmmmmmmmmmmmmmmmmmmmmmmm
mmmmmm|             |mmmmmmmmmmmmmmmmmmmmmmmmmmm
mmmmmm\            /mmmmmmmmmmmmmmmmmmmmmmmmmm
=======       ====================
=====================================
mmmmmmmmmmmmmmmmmmmmmmmmmmmmmmmmmmmmmmmmmmmmmmmmmm
```

                    OTIS
          Oh.
          (beat)
          You're sort of, nice-looking?

                  ANEURYSM
          I knew you'd come around.

8. INT. DOCTOR'S OFFICE - EARLY EVENING -
   FLASHBACK

The doctor absentmindedly circles a blood-test
result.

> DOCTOR
> There's a chance the clot will
> never burst, then it would be
> irresponsible for me to oper-
> ate - it could kill you. But
> if it isn't controllable, if
> the clot could cause a rup-
> ture, it would be irresponsi-
> ble for me not to operate - it
> could kill you.

9. INT. LATE-SHIFT BUS - BACK TO THE PRESENT

Otis looks at his watery reflection in the bus
window. The streetlights pass, fast now, strobing
his worry-crumpled brow.

OTIS' REFLECTION (-26), like Otis but cooler-
looking, straightens. It pulls up its nose in
disgust.

> OTIS' REFLECTION
> Your half of the universe is
> so pathetic. Get it together.

Otis looks around, desperate for confirmation that
somebody else on the bus can see his reflection
gone rogue.

> BUS RADIO
> ...I'll be your mirror, re-
> flect what you are, in case you
> don't know...

Otis' reflection rolls its eyes.

                    OTIS' REFLECTION
          Really? You think night-school-
          dropout and office-security over
          here are going to help you?
                    (beat)
          Your universe is about to divide.
          You've got bigger problems.

Otis' reflection snaps its fingers. The window pane
ripples and shifts into infinitely big circles,
then tugs violently at the edges of itself.

The world splits in half.

INT. THE FIRST UNIVERSE   INT. THE SECOND UNIVERSE
- LATE BUS - CONTINUOUS   - LATE BUS - CONTINUOUS

          ANEURYSM   ANEURYSM
Why are we on this bus,   Why are we on this bus,
Otis?   Otis?

            OTIS   OTIS
I'm getting rid of you.   I'm going to call off
                                 the surgery.

          ANEURYSM
Really? I'm everything   ANEURYSM
you ever wanted to be.   You're going to let a
I'm your body finally   little blood take you
standing up for itself.   out?
You want to bleed like
it's an apology? Or is   OTIS
there finally something   I figure I'm okay with
unyielding in your veins?   it.

043

OTIS

It's the best chance
I've got. Nothing per-
sonal. Sorry, Aneurysm.

ANEURYSM

Chance? Forget it.
Every chance splits
the universe, like the
veins in your head, but
they all end in the
same place. You die.

OTIS
  (chuckling)
That's something a
deadly blood clot would
say.

ANEURYSM

You can't know what'll
kill you. Let's call
a truce. Just because
some medical text-
book says it'll be me,
doesn't mean it won't
be this bus.

ANEURYSM

After all you've been
through?

OTIS

Come on, you know how
this ends, a little
blood was always going
to take me out. Ever
scraped your knee and
nearly bled out?

ANEURYSM

I'm a figment of your
imagination, I don't
have knees.

OTIS

I suppose you don't.

ANEURYSM

Will you tell everyone
I was a good aneurysm?

OTIS

What do you mean?

ANEURYSM

I'm not even going to
be the thing that kills
you. Isn't that crazy?
(beat)
Hey Otis, are you even
paying attention to the
bus?

10. INT. LATE BUS - CONTINUOUS

The two halves of the world struggle for domi-
nance, their edges pressing against one another.
Then, just as quickly as they split, they merge.
Otis wrings his hands out in an attempt to shake
off the strangeness of being split in half. It
doesn't work, of course, being divided and hastily
re-merged is a quantum discomfort.

                    OTIS
          What about the bus?
          What's wrong with the bus?

The traffic light turns orange.

                    OTIS
          Aneurysm?
          No response.

The bus driver shakes his wrinkly fist and curses
at the, now-certainly-broken-down, hatchback which
has failed to move.

                    OTIS
          Why did we merge? Why are we
          back on the same path?

The driver puts the parking brake down.
The bus heaves with a great pneumatic whoosh.
Pulls into the oncoming lane.

                    OTIS
          Aneurysm? Come back, please?

A medical supply truck, coming fast.

Inevitable.

                              CUT TO BLACK

11. INT./EXT. OTIS'S BRAIN/ENDLESS SPACE –
    CONTINUOUS/TIMELESS

ANEURYSM, a pinkish clump of cells, like a de-
formed jelly baby. OTIS, a blueish clump of consciousness, like a wadded up tissue.

The pair float like plastic bags on the wind, like
dancers. They stretch out a tendril towards one
another, connect, come to rest in the air.

> OTIS
>
> Where are we?

> ANEURYSM
>
> We're in your brain.
> (beat)
> Not like that, though. You're
> not having thoughts.

> OTIS
>
> Am I dead?

> ANEURYSM
>
> Likely.

A comfortable silence passes, Otis's blue light
flickers and dims a little.

> OTIS
>
> I can't believe I died in a
> bus accident.

> ANEURYSM
>
> Don't worry about it. Sometimes
> the choices make themselves.

A beat.

> CUT TO BLACK

Coagulation: A Tribute

Jarred Thompson

Some people live whole lives with an aneurysm
as their question, pear-shaped and posed

in every vessel there is turbulence—living-little-Lego pieces
are the clot, the geometry

of healing, bought in currencies of
shape binding tumult to silence. Blood is a jelly

responsive to caesuras in its sentences, the forces spent
trading sweat for money, reshuffling rivers

in the basins of our brain, forming islands
where once I was a bird, absorbed in a dreamscape

suddenly branched, broken, born
from a womb, with a brain whose horizons

are rivers, millimetres thick: the time it takes to think

your blood, and summon pacts made
with mangled facts—the lineage of bodies

opening into you. Time's living test tube turned valid
through failure, verified through fantasy.

How do you warm the territories furthest from
the heart's centre, if you don't pressure past chasms

to gather here, on this craggy outpost
of fibrin, and sleeve off for the beloved,

that charges at you, like a greyhound in the road,
curious to meet your panting with its tongue.

It Comes from Nowhere

Zanta Nkumane

Suddenly, I am sprawled everywhere on the ground and slivers of crimson run down my leg. The stream flows fast, warm and can't densify because the liquor flowing inside it has made it thin. I curse myself, and God – always God too – for my clumsiness. I pull myself up. I hazily check if my phone isn't damaged and decide I will dress the wound when I get home. Under the dim lights of a bare street, I drip tiny red moons onto the tar all the way home.

I am a clumsy drunk. My legs become leaden with every drink. My judgement becomes distorted and my body's affinity for smashing into things, people and the ground surges with each tequila shot. My arms and legs have become scar-maps charting the weekend nights I only half-remember. I've found unexpected comfort tending to them over the years because the steps are clear and work every time – stop the bleeding, disinfect and, depending on the depth of the wound, a bandage. Then the body works its intricate healing process. And time – always time too.

I wish tending to my heartbreak was as undemanding and foolproof as dressing a scrape or a cut after falling. I wish it was rather a gaping wound that I could balm and bandage. Over time, I'd watch it weave itself back into a tissue integrity similar to before the heartbreak came.

But heartbreak doesn't work like that.

***

When I was twenty-one, my appendix ruptured. Before that, I am unclear if my body had experienced trauma of that immensity, besides grief. That repair took months on my body. Even longer on my mind because this inexplicable shame of my fairly young body failing me in that manner haunted me. This scar that looks like a trunk of a big tree with its bark peeled, skews down from the navel to above my crotch. It arches so long because once the appendix ruptures, it releases toxins into your system. They fling open your gut to clean it all out and leave your body to its healing devices. And prayer – always prayer too. After the pins were removed, I tended the wound obsessively, like it was a floret. Wiping it down tenderly, ensuring that I didn't strain my body too much in case it tore open and sometimes never letting lovers see me naked in the light.

My first true adult heartbreak happened that same year too. But that healing process was neither as coordinated nor successful as my body's. It was a cesspool of emotions I didn't know how to process and recover from. I had met him a few months after my operation. He was devastatingly quick-witted and unpretentious. He wore brightly coloured cardigans and didn't seem like he was trying too hard. His spirit was robust enough to not fold too fast but pliable enough to learn without feeling like he was losing something. A few months into what I thought was a committed romance, I saw him kiss someone else. A flood of needles rushed into my chest, inflaming it in a way that felt bigger than me. I am not sure how we feel new things, but when my bubble was burst by that first heartbreak, it was also as if I had never felt anything before that moment. It discoloured my world and also rendered it more vivid as I discovered that feeling could stretch further than myself. That whole-body yearning, desperate to fold in on itself in devastated, defensive embrace is reminiscent of how the body initiates inflammatory signals that cause more blood to flow to a traumatised area. This rush of blood delivers the necessary components to start the healing process. After an injury, the body will form clots to prevent more blood loss, and underneath that layer of protection a cascade of reparative processes are active. Without blood, there's no healing. There have been many heartbreaks since that first one, all different in their magnitude. But each time I have had to invent my own healing process. Mine lacks the tidiness of the body's process, because not only am I a clumsy drunk – I can be clumsy with my heart too. My heartbreak cascade, albeit not foolproof, tends to be set in motion by the devastation/anguish. Such emotion initiates the vital lachrymal cycle. My brain sympathetically reaches out to the lachrymal apparatus, encouraging the glands to produce tears which are homed in the tear ducts. Overwhelmed by the excess, the ducts relinquish their integrity, and so I quietly spill. I strongly recommend crying, through joy and pain because they're our feelings in potion form. Tears are transformative. They demarcate the before and the after of an event. They portal you into a soothing, whether immediate or slow burning. Without tears, there's no healing. Then a bevy of playlists, for different moods. Recovery is not linear and a wide variety of sounds to match your haphazard moods can be helpful. Some days, I am rippling with bitterness and other days, my chest wants to shred away from my body because it cannot bear the feeling. One morning I'm wailing to Prince's 'Nothing Compares 2 U'; by the afternoon swaying to Joan Armatrading's 'Love and Affection' and by the evening seeking comfort in Moonchild's 'The Other Side'. As tears are liquefied feeling, so music echoes feeling. And dancing – always dancing too.

The intangibility of heartbreak makes it cumbersome. It can seem incurable because only time makes it more bearable. Broken hearts are difficult to remedy because there isn't a prescription that works for all of us. But even then, heartbreak is something you feel everywhere and nowhere. Takotsubo cardiomyopathy – broken heart syndrome – is a reparable condition common in women. It presents as a weakening of the left ventricle due to extreme physical or emotional stress like death, illness or "receiving bad news", etc. Even so, Takotsubo cardiomyopathy is the rare example of a correlation of heartbreak with a physical manifestation. I imagine that after being treated and discharged, the patient remains with the unsettling feeling of heartbreak. For me, it's this unreachable lingering heartbreak which proves most wearisome to address. There'll never be enough drunken nights. The unembodied portion seems the most potent ailment to heal from. At times I wonder if our own were as majestic as the hearts of blue whales, maybe that enormity would render our feelings voluminous enough, transmuting into physical matter we could excise.

If I ever encounter the entity responsible for the creation of this world, a stern talking-to will be deserved. For, in devising intricate somatic healing processes, how could they have neglected to endow our broken hearts the same?

11

Poems

Jerome Coetzee

Overdrive

There are forces applied
to women
Your actions describe
women as objects
Inflicting multiple injuries
This country should be
in overdrive to heal

These actions cannot be washed out
Cannot be dissolved
Women
injured without cuts
How can you not
understand this disease?

They should be visualised
beyond the numbers

This country
has a high risk of rupture
Blood vessels boiling
like inflating balloons
This is not a random chaotic movement

Regenerate

I have died a long time ago,
my body parts have faded at different stages,
I joined my ancestors in this state,
parts of my body have gone
without oxygen
and need
materials that can flow
and yet is solid.
The rest of my body is strained,
wanting to live and keep going,
pumping the blood,
awakening the power to regenerate the tissues.
Trying to convince the dead parts that life is
worth coming back from the dead for.
These dead tissues remind me
every day that they were mismatched
within every space
and choosing life
would be losing a simple right to die.
In the end, dead tissue is still covered,
covered in skin that moves
within the spaces of the living.

12

Fractals

Wamuwi Mbao

There is a time between the happening and the registering when nothing is wrong. Sometimes the registering is quick, and sometimes there is no registering at all. When JFK was shot the first time, he turned in his seat, a registering of danger like what happens when a wasp stings you. What follows horrifies. How magnetism can be snuffed out. How the human becomes meat, raw, bloodied, suddenly expressed as finitude. Blood is what keeps the humanity circulating.

Heart. Stop. The blood triangle. What stops blood getting out. How quickly it leaves. Sometimes the stopping is the problem. Sometimes there is a lack of stopping. This can be deadly. Sometimes the lack of stopping is the problem. Sometimes the stopping slows, and the slowing is the problem. The slowing is the thing. Slowing kills.

For a time, I am intrigued by things that happen in short durations.

When John Lennon was shot on a New York street in December 1980, he remained alive for long enough to have staggered into the lobby of an apartment building named the Dakota. He would have had time to observe, before he lost consciousness, that he was dying, and that nobody was coming to save him. The bullet that killed him had damaged his body in a way that meant it could not repair itself.

***

Marilyn Monroe's autopsy picture doesn't look like the Marilyn we think we know. The hair is not in the configuration we associate with her. The wispy curls lie flat on her scalp. The organisation it had in life is no longer there.

When people write about Marilyn Monroe, you sense that there's a desire to want to make her a bodied thing. We're uncomfortable with people unless we can see what makes them human. Think of all the peroxide. Women don't look like that today. How much do you think she weighed?

***

Everyone hopes for a good death, whatever they take that to mean. They usually mean, a death free from the humiliations that so often come with death. Having one's skull knocked in by a falling object. The heart giving out on the toilet. Dying in the office, after hours, overtime and out of time.

Death is deeply unoriginal. Occasionally funny. Unintentionally so, sometimes, like realising that the laugh track for an old sitcom is a kind of hauntography.

***

An accident is a coming-together of variables to create one fixed calamity. Something slips out of place, someone forgets the choreography, and the whole thing jars. Eyes, ears, mouths all allow the blood to escape. I once saw someone who'd come out of his car as it rolled over. You wouldn't believe a body could do that, put itself so thoroughly beyond saving like that.

***

While we are in this workshop at the foot of a mountain range in the Western Cape, the incumbent British Prime minister is trying to retain control as it slips from his grasp. His being is characterised by a certain rumpled jocularity, emphasised by a disorganised mop of blonde hair. The hair is often read, obliquely or directly, as being redolent of his term in office. His hair is part of a strategy. It enables him to weather most challenges. But it also anticipates his inevitable ruination. It contains a story within itself. When he goes, the usual photo of the departing no-longer will be the last glimpse of a particular configuration of government. Whoever replaces him will be neater, and the neatness will relieve anxiety.

I might ask myself later if a neater hairstyle would have saved him.

***

When I walk around town, I know that I'm due for a haircut when Rastafarians start greeting me. I can judge my weight fluctuations by who they think I look like. It's bad when I'm the rugby player. It's good when I'm the DJ or the comedian. Once, and only once, someone thought I was the guy from Bloc Party. I've spent a lifetime trying to get back there.

***

Keeping yourself alive is about retaining as much of your native functionality as possible. Sometimes the odds are against you. When I was fifteen, I heard someone say that if John Lennon had been shot in an emergency room and collapsed onto a bed, the doctors there still would not have been able to save him.

Twenty years after that fact was relayed to me by VH1, I take pills that keep my blood as close to its default configuration as is possible. From this experience, I have borne away the idea that every time I felt my heart failing to play its part, the thing I'm feeling may itself be a form of ending.

***

One of us takes a walk up the hillside. The sun is shining slowly upon the green grass and we are mumbling pleasantries. We see the shade and long for the in-between. In the day, when it is sunny and midwinter, it is nice to sit still and wait for significant things to happen. We are gathered to talk about the processes that animate the body. We discuss shoes and the mechanics of meat. The light fades and there are new social circulations. The world feels far away. A bark echoes down the canyon. The propensity for mist makes us feel unsafe.

***

What fascinates me about the Manson murders is that – like many viscerally violent acts in society – they expose the fantasy of the human as a permeable construction. A house is architecture, but when poorly defended, it could become an abbatoir. A group of friends arranged for an evening is a social construct that ceases to have meaning when all the blood is let out.

Afterwards, there are proscriptions on details, and a strange black-market trade emerges in autopsy photos because people are fascinated by the misfortunes of others. At least it wasn't me. That's not my blood on that wall. It seems profane, how close the human is to being meat. It starts with an unlocked door.

***

We all have the same concerns. Will there be someone to sit with? Will I be able to contribute to the flow of conversation?

You live from city (Systole) to town (diastole). The highway carries red droplet taillights along the dark artery. Here is a way to go. Here is the circulation. There are a great many public information films devoted to the idea that with good sense, the body can be kept whole and unpunctured. Observe following distances. Wear a seat belt. Don't speed. In the home, too. Use a ladder. Don't rush. Don't use an angle grinder or a Stanley knife or a guillotine or an axe or a lawnmower without remembering to keep yourself alive.

***

One has a brief period of time before the body begins to behave like an overripe fruit.

***

A body drops from the pedestrian overpass at its highest point, breaking itself against the tar. The dropping and the breaking cause traffic to halt where it leaves the city. The clot needs to be cleared, and so for thirty minutes the cars stand in impatient tribute to the stopped body. By dropping, the body has ceased to be an idea (for that's what people are) and become instead an exhibition of brains and blood and teeth (there's one, over there).

***

Our anxieties around aging express themselves as a concern with the minute twinges the body makes as its workings expand or contract. A fear of exposure, a fear of not-working that takes root and becomes permanent, a sense that the last sharp zing could herald the great disordering. Clinging on in quiet desperation. Not just an English thing, *pace* Pink Floyd.

The easing of that sudden pain is a second chance. Tomorrow, we will say no to the bacon. Tomorrow we will not have rice, or too much of everything. If we wear those sporty shoes, then we will keep death out of our bloodstream. So it goes.

***

He does not know if these droplets of narrative will coagulate. They have burrs that catch on each other, momentarily or over a prolonged time. We take advantage of science to be creative. The creative can be personal, an opportunity to take the personal and put it out into the world. We are all trying to be someone else. The outline stays more or less the same, but the content changes. I am suspicious of the drive to find something of oneself in everything. It creeps in liquidly, a murmur like water across a floor. We steer away from unbearable earnestness. The desire to make the self fruitful.

13

Always in Motion

Alistair Mackay

He tells her she can call him Trevor. "Like the comedian," he says, which she seems to find very funny. It's partially a joke – he knows he comes across as serious and withdrawn – but it's also just easier. Easy to remember. Easier than telling her anything real about himself.

"You have resting-wise-face," she declares. She's drunk, and apparently very proud of her coinage. She sighs theatrically and collapses against the back seat in a heap of blonde curls. He lets himself feel warm for a second, and relaxed. Maybe that will be the end of the talking. But then she leans forward and says, "Since you're so wise, what do you think I should do about ..." and proceeds to tell him all about her ex, whom she ran into tonight, and was there still chemistry there, because there shouldn't be, they fought so much when they were together, that's why they had an on-again, off-again relationship, and Trevor feels the pressure build behind his eyes, and it makes him angry – the pressure to not only listen to this story he isn't interested in, but to actually *be* wise, and say something thoughtful and uplifting because she feels entitled to it, and it suits her conception of him. And why? She'll have forgotten about this whole conversation, and his existence, by the time she sobers up, and she isn't nearly as distraught as she thinks she is, either. It's all empty words. This is what Trevor's nephew would call 'content' – the stuff that fills up conversations and social media.

He can tell, even with all of her complaining and drama, that she believes things will be fine in the end. And she's right. Things are always fine for people like her. She doesn't need reassurance, but she wants it. (*This*, Trevor's nephew would call 'emotional labour'.) She has that quality that people who have known security in their childhoods exude. An expectation of support. He'd seen her slur-shout her goodbyes at her friends when he picked her up outside the bar in Illovo, and watched her fall into his car like she knew it would catch her. Even if her romance fails, she has her people.

"Where are you from, Trevor?" she asks, when he hasn't said anything in a while.

"No, I live here," he replies, and she seems satisfied with that.

After he's dropped her off at an apartment block in Killarney, things are quiet for a while. There are no ride requests. He pulls over on a side street near the bridge over the freeway. He loves these city arteries at night. Especially at sunset, in winter, this freeway works better than almost anything else to keep the dread at bay. The city is a living, breathing thing. Alive with heavy metals in the blood. Ten thousand golden headlights flood northwards in the arteries. The spent, glittering embers of red taillights pull southwards in parallel veins towards the heart. He can hear the heart, the whole vascular system. A deep, steady hum of traffic, of living, thumping up against the sky, reverberating in his chest. He is near the heart of the city now. The old diseased, ramshackle, resilient one. The other heart is further north. Marbled, gilded and soulless. What kind of monster has two hearts?

All the better to keep the darkness at bay.

Except, it's too late now. A few long-haul trucks and ride-share drivers. Blood flow has slowed right down. The monster is asleep.

If Trevor can move, the darkness isn't so frightening. If he's moving, it means he isn't trapped at home, stuck waiting, listening for when they come for him. In his car, he is invisible. He is free. A tiny speck in the bloodstream. No one knows where he is. No one knows who he is. Even if hijackers come, he has his accelerator. Their attacks aren't personal. They won't hunt him down. They will simply turn their violence onto someone else.

The downside of working the late night trips is that many of his passengers are drunk. Sometimes it's not so bad. They joke and laugh and sing, they tease one another, and he feels buoyed by their spirits, but sometimes they shout at him or demand he find good music, and turn it up. They argue with him over routes. Twice, he's had someone vomit. Once in his car, and it took weeks to get the smell out. Bitter and acidic. He's still not sure he ever got the stain out completely.

Still, he reminds himself: it's better than what he left behind.

His second trip of the night is a couple in their fifies. It's a restaurant pick-up and the couple was the last to leave. Trevor knows this because he watches the waiters stack the chairs on the tables through the restaurant windows as the couple gets into his car. He feels annoyed that the two of them were chased out because they are so obviously still in love, and it's a miracle to see love like this, a bright glittering light in the darkness, and for the restaurant staff to be so unmoved, so impatient, debases the whole thing. The couple's love is not new. Trevor can see this immediately. They are very familiar with one another, very comfortable. There is none of the tension of the unexpected between them; but there is no boredom, either. No disdain.

It's too dark in the car for Trevor to see if there are wedding bands on their fingers; but, in his rearview mirror, he glimpses the husband – for he wants to imagine he is her husband – taking the woman's hand in his own. She smiles, softly, and the two of them watch the city rush past on either side of their respective windows like dark fluid. Trevor imagines their children at home – two boys, maybe teenagers by now, fighting and teasing each other like his brother used to do with him – and he almost asks them if they have children, but he does not want to find out that they are childless, or that this is a side-relationship or anything that would ruin this moment. He also does not like to talk too much because it's never long before his passengers' questions turn to his own life, and what is there to say about that which wouldn't leave the taste of metal in his mouth?

He drops the couple off at a home in Parkwood and proceeds to Melville, where he accepts a good, long ride with decent fare.

At first, he does not see the blood on them. The darkness plays tricks on him. Shadows everywhere, cast from the glowing signs of the bars in Melville. The men position themselves so that the light fails to catch their injuries until it's too late. By the time Trevor realises that the darkness on the one man's forehead is not a shadow but blood seeping from a gash, the man is already inside his car and the door is closed. His friend comes around the vehicle to the other side and Trevor thinks, for a second, that the man is going to drag him out of his seat. That's what happened to that Uber driver in Katlehong, isn't it? They dragged him out his vehicle, whipped him, destroyed his car, and kidnapped him in their taxi. Was he ever found?

"You must get out," Trevor says. "I can't take you."

"Relax," the first passenger says, catching Trevor's eye in the rear-view mirror. "I won't get blood on anything." He does not move to get out.

The second passenger falls into the back seat and he, too, is bleeding. Gashes on his forearms and below his cheekbone. Trevor's chest has tightened and his own blood is cold. His senses have misfired, again, and reality drains from him. What's left where reality should be is too bright and too loud and yet also very, very far away.

"What happened to you?"

"This was just an accident. We fell." Trevor watches them in the mirror for as long as he can. He is sweating. He needs to know if they were the victims or the aggressors. These are not the wounds of a fall. Why would they lie to him? Are they ashamed of what happened? Humiliated? Or are they the most frightening of all violent men – the kind who smile at you and tell you to relax, who say thank you. The ones with a softness around the eyes.

Trevor summons all the strength he has left in his body to push back up into this world from where he's fallen, that cold, far away place. He tries to say *no,* again, to say *I can't take you,* but the only word that comes out is: "Hospital?"

"We don't need a hospital," says the less drunk of the two. And then, to placate the driver, he winks and says "Thanks. Just the address I entered on the app."

"Trev," the other one says, "let's go, let's go."

Trevor puts the car into gear and pulls away. He tries to imagine all that blood as a kind of tree sap. His grandfather used to bleed trees when he was a young man, back in the rural village Trevor visited sometimes with his parents. They still do it in those parts of the continent – which have never felt further away than they do right now – for palm wine and rubber. They slice into living tree flesh and the blood runs out and the villagers catch the life within them, and yet everything is okay. The trees do not die. They withstand the violence. They offer their insides and those insides don't smell like death or fear. Trevor tries to imagine a clean, sweet smell. A bite of succulent mango, its juice running down the chin.

It does not work. "Do you mind if I open the window a little?"

One of them makes a dismissive hand gesture that Trevor takes to mean, *do whatever you like*. They are heading west and picking up speed and an open window makes the swirling, thundering air hurt his ears, but it also gets rid of the smell. And it makes their conversation impossible to hear, which is a relief. He had been straining to hear their subdued, conspiratorial murmuring – did he understand the language? Did he recognise it? *Now he is set free.*

But his body remembers, even if his mind retreats.

The adrenaline tingles in his blood. He can still feel it, the memory trapped within each and every cell, the paralysis of being surrounded. The defeat of having run and run and run, and not escaped. The words they used to justify their hatred – foreigner, *makwerekwere* – were so different from the words they used back home, but the hatred was the same. Thousands of kilometres away and yet here too, the mob. When the rock struck his brother, it was as if Trevor felt it in his own body, his whole body. And then the blood. Pouring from his brother's broken nose, and then, with the second strike, from his eye. Trevor's knees went weak. Was *he* losing blood? Had he also been struck? For a second, he wanted to be, he wanted to share this with his brother so that his brother didn't have to bear it alone, so that neither of them were alone in this terror.

And then he was hit, too, already on his way down into the sandy dirt. He thought, why is there so much blood? He thought, all we are is blood. There is so little to hold us in, to keep us from pouring out into the earth. Leaking out through our perforated casing. We behave like blood, too. Clotting to protect. Sealing shut to heal a wound. Mobs and family, both. We congeal. An unspoken chain reaction of white blood cells to drive out invaders, proteins and platelets to knit an impenetrable blockade. But why do these people perceive a wound? What did he or his brother ever do to injure anybody?

Trevor will do anything, anything, to not think of his family right now.

They are entering a part of the city that's unfamiliar to Trevor. The small, broken veins of roads far from the organs and arteries. Blood flow is slow here in the periphery of the great sprawling monster. Clots are easy to form. He pulls the car over, opens his door, leans out and heaves his insides into the dirt.

"Are you drunk?" one of the passengers says from behind him, and Trevor has to laugh. All of these drunk passengers every night and they think he is the drunk? He laughs despite the acid all over his lips. Trevor, the comedian.

He wipes his mouth. He gets out of the car, and opens the back door. "Get out," he says.

The two men look at him. "We're not there yet," says the one with cuts on his arms. He is outraged, but his friend is not. Trevor knows that expression all too well. His friend, the one with the gash on his forehead, is terrified. "Please," the friend says. His voice is small. "Please."

Trevor closes the door and gets back into the driver's seat. They might be brothers, but Trevor can't bear to ask them. No one speaks for a long time. He starts the engine. He turns on the sound system. He never listens to music when he has passengers, in case they ask him where it's from. But these passengers don't say anything about the music. They don't say anything at all. No conspiratorial whispering. Nothing to upset Trevor. Trevor wants to laugh again, and shake himself like a dog after a fight, but he knows how frightening laughter can be. And the fight is only in his cells.

No one is getting expelled or attacked tonight, at least. The two-hearted monster sleeps. Trevor drives the two bloodied men home.

14

Artefacts

Mika Conradie

She did not want to know, but she has since come to know that the river, long before she was born, was directed and dammed over the graves of men dead.

Not so long before that her ancestors were, at the time, much further north. But they were on their way, they were coming to the river.

They arrived and, some time after their arrival, were buried next to the river which was at a time after that damned.

***

["What is time?"]¹

***

---

1   The character Zabou asks in *Timbuktu* (2014), directed by Mauritanian filmmaker Abderrahmane Sissako, as she measures the historical length and breadth of occupation as disaster.

18—,

a Dutch man comes to find a name for the river. !Ha!arib is its indigenous name. He translates this to the muscle-memory of his tongue – *Vaal Rivier*.

Pale River, *Restrained* River, *Muted* River.

(In time, may the river forget these names and remember its first.)

Then.
A German man comes to draw borders and thinks fondly of his time in Paris. *This* river would be his Seine.
He spits his memory into it.

There crawls *Parys,* a small town on the edge of the Muted River.

***

1992,

Mimosa is the name of the manicured resort that borders a small tributary. The tributary is a jagged scratch that pulls down against the skin of the town, all the way to the river.
　The park beckons with its waterpark slides.
　She cannot afford the entrance, so her grandmother sets the picnic down outside the gates, on the grassy island in the centre of the parking lot.

[*tributary; from Latin* tributarius, *from* tributum; *of* tribuere *'to assign' originally 'divide between tribes', see also tribute: a testimony, or tax, or a eulogy*].

She presses her face against the chicken-wire fence, letting the metal emboss her skin with small red diamonds. She watches other children fly down the slides,

with,
in,
and through artificial rapids.

[I can swim just like the others. Only I have a better memory than the others. I have not forgotten the former inability to swim. But since I have not forgotten it, being able to swim is of no help to me; and so, after all, I cannot swim.][2]

Her failure to swim does not stop her from having something to reach for, but what she reaches for may not remember her.

***

Reaching:

19—,

there is a very large public swimming pool, a bit of a ways out
of town, which always feels like a special occasion –
perhaps a new year's thing.
And save that, a large tin bucket, that she can lie in from head
to toe, a toddler, in the back of an overgrown garden with another
river-scratch creating a boundary.
And an old woman with a cup of water in her hand and the
repetition of water over hair into tub and water into cup over hair
into tub so that very night she is baptised in a shallow
of warm river water.

***

Memory is a river which is a water-knot, picking up and laying down debris inconstantly, from connecting estuaries, confluences,

---

2   Quoted in Aaron Schuster "Kafka Swims: Champion of the Impossible" in *Cabinet*, 28 May 2020.

tributaries. The material culture of a river is endless and cannot be anticipated.

It carries wild artefacts. It is wild artefact.

***

1995,

She is 5 years old and must cross the river. Her mother has come to fetch her to the city. Across the bridge is school.

Before she crosses, she holds her grandmother.

Her body is approximately 67% water.

Her grandmother's body is approximately 67% water.

They leak some of this percentage as they cry. Water transfers from the old woman's eyes to the child's face, from the child's eyes to the old woman's face.

As she crosses the river, she closes her palms against her cheeks, trapping the water in her skin. Her face bloats with grief,
    a grief that holds like water damage.

    The river borders memory, and also holds memory.
    The shore is both waterlogged and adjacent to water.

***

The freshwater littoral is the area near the river-shore that is submerged, floating, or emergent. It is an area that is always imminent.

Always shifting, memory is the river-
littoral.

[Occasionally the river floods these places.
'Floods' is the word they use, but in fact it is not flooding; it is remembering.
Remembering where it used to be.][3]

***

Artefact is not related to *artery*, but artefacts can be found in arteries.

No, they cannot be found in arteries:

in biomechanical terms an artefact is a visual representation of a thing that does not actually exist in the object being represented:

it is a speck of dust on the MRI.
Or it is a ghost, a shadow that is formed on the photograph if you move while your body is being scanned.
Or the visual representation of a loss of signal.

This is termed 'spatial misregistration'.

***

2012,

she almost drives off the road into river reeds. The banks of her eyes have burst and she cannot see where she is going. Eyes make for weak embankments, but there has been another flood: an artery in the heart of her grandmother breaks its bounds.

What did the blood remember?
Where did the blood try to remember to?

***

---

3   Toni Morrison, From a talk given at the New York Public Library in 1986.

Sluices are carved between the street and pavement. When she was a child, she was allowed to swim in these little rivers, but now they are empty. The town has learnt to modernise its management of water.

It's all subterranean now, streamlined to a river of pipes. She walks around the town urging a recollection of something. She wants to swim, but she wades.

When she looks at the furrows in the pavement she thinks of water and its management,

[*shaped, diverted, bifurcated, narrowed, shortened, widened, channelled, straightened,*
   dredged,
   deepened,
   damned,

Redirected, embanked, canalised.][4]

All ways to think memory too.

***

Another way to think memory:

2020,

Graves break the line of water with fists of stone.
   More wild
artefact: stone has learnt to breathe under water. First forced to flood and damning land, the river now pulls back to remember where it once was, revealing the concealed. The things the river knows is equivalent to what she does not know. The things the dead remember, equivalent to what the river knows.

***

---

4   Matt Edgeworth, *Fluid Pasts: Archaeology of Flow*, p. 14. London: Bloomsbury Academic, 2011.

15

Unrooted

Alistair Mackay

We are not so different
Veins branching blood-red through late-summer leaves
And in our eyes, when the ophthalmologist's light is blinding.
Fluid flows through our organs
And for them – rises from the earth in xylem
to be exhaled.
We shed our skin
in chips and scales and dust
and our blood congeals
a sticky resin on bark.
Are we the objects or the subject
of consciousness?
Who is observing whom?
A secret language of whispers and rustling;
Warnings secreted through chemicals
in the soil
in the breeze
If you pay attention
you will still miss it
but maybe you will sense what you are missing.
They scar, too.

Trees remember droughts and disease,
and axes,
saws and knives
the violence of names (and hearts) carved into their living flesh.
Do we remember what it was like
before we learned not to hear
before we unrooted ourselves
and decided we were alone?

16

Notes on Boundary and Flow

Mehita Iqani

Inside

Inside this body right here, beneath this skin I mean, is a skeleton. Attached to those bones are muscles, are tendons and ligaments; housed within this ribcage are lungs and a heart and several other organs (minus an appendix, which recently got slurped out through my belly button, just like other writers in this group). Connecting all of these are a network of vessels. Arteries and veins that carry blood around, oxygenated from the heart and de-oxygenated in the other direction. Nerves that transmit constant, complex instructions back and forth from the brain. This much we know from school biology, from Wikipedia, from the anatomy app I downloaded to better point out muscles to physiotherapists.

Inside this body right here is a structure so complex and detailed that, when I stop to think about it, I am quickly congested, intellectually speaking.

I cannot look within myself as much as I cannot cast an eye over the dark side of the moon.

Zoom in. Look right into the centre of the tiniest blood vessel. Examine its dimensions. Measure the rate at which a fluid can pass through. Map the movement of that fluid and represent it on X and Y axes. Create a computer model that predicts what will happen to the rate of movement if a certain protein is added or removed from the fluid. Plot it on the graph again. Keep doing this until your graph looks like a rainbow.

Consider how passage may be blocked, and further, how an obstruction may be removed. Plot all the configurations of blockage and gush on to a chart, then colour code the variations. Choose red for one end of the continuum and blue for the other. Carry on until the image looks like an abstract oil painting.

Apart from how this body feels, right here, right now (Do I have a headache? Am I thirsty? Have I overeaten? Am I sluggish from lack of movement? Did I manage to sleep last night?), everything that happens inside of it is just a narrative to me. Scientist needs to explain the story of how the heart pumps the blood, gesturing into the air with a jerky, pacing, rhythmic hand motion, to show how it constricts and releases. Someone needs to name elements as actors and substances as subjects and suggest to me a plot about what drives their behaviour and what they are compelled to do next.

Everything becomes a metaphor. Experiments tell stories. Equations are named to be remembered. Under my skin: a city with functioning roads and railways, passages and sewers, highways and rivers ferrying things busily this way and that. If I could send in a microscopic explorer submarine, would it be able to travel all the routes before I died?

Inside the organic geometry of this body, this tissue, this blood, this force and mass: solids and fluids interact as governed by universal laws. Holding together something known as me.

Flow

"How do you guys work with the notion of truth?" I ask. It's more of a comment than a question because I follow it up with the explanation that from my epistemological positioning, truth is always relative, always subjective. Scientist has mentioned a couple times that they always have to "test if their models are true."

When we observe the same thing enough times, we can ascertain that there is a certain law in operation, she replies. A *universal* law. Universal laws are *true*.

I sit back and try to accept this. How many times is enough? I do not dispute that, for example, on planet earth, things fall downwards. Even balloons, eventually. I agree that water is comprised of two hydrogen molecules and one oxygen, because this what I have been taught. To someone working with mechanics, there are physical laws that govern how substances can move in this universe. Substance A, of a Viscosity B, can move in only a limited number of ways in Condition C. These behaviours have been figured out through close observation, experiments, more observation, cross-checking, and increasingly, computer modelling.

I scribble in my notes:

Flow. The keyword for all this science is FLOW.

Hardly an epiphany! Scientist specialises in fluid mechanics and has been talking to us for three days about how blood clots, or doesn't, when a liquid turns to a gel upon injection into heart tissue, and the elastic properties of hair fibres. But still, I feel that I am touching something pure, not only in my own understanding but beyond it, something universal that exists apart from me: FLOW. My eureka moment quickly passes to sheepishness about the yoga-hippy connotations flow and connection catchphrases.

"I am rooted, but I flow." "Equanimity is the balance between effort and ease." "You can never step in the same river twice."

Is the humanities brain nothing more than an index of catchy clichés?

I am humbled by graphs and snapshots of microscopy slides. The superpower that can see inside blood vessels the width of a single strand of hair. The code that can model the same without slicing into flesh.

I clutch on to the truism that fluid mechanics is all about flow. Perhaps it is all I will ever understand. Perhaps it is enough.

Outside

When I was twenty-three-ish, I attended a yoga class for the first time, awkwardly occupying shapes, some of which would later become as familiar as pyjamas. I couldn't touch my toes at all; my fingers reached just around about the middle of my shins. But I liked it, the stretching. After a childhood filled with not much sport, I had little body awareness and lived mostly in my head, the face of which was usually buried in a book. Making shapes while breathing taught me to consider the extent and reach of my own body, and to see myself as a physical being as well as an abstract aggregate of ideas and emotions.

Ah, I remember thinking, *this* is where my fingertips end! I could feel precisely into their exact length and dimensions. I started to experience the amount of space that I took up and noticed the edges of myself. Beyond this, everything else. Within this, *me*.

Decades later, I am asked what yoga has brought to my life. I think of that aha moment and answer confidently that yoga demonstrates where the body ends, and the rest of the world begins.

Yes, the guru muses, yes indeed. Where *does* your body end? Where *does* the rest of the world begin?

I am confused. My statement is surely so obviously true as to warrant nothing more than congratulatory agreement. Correct: physical practices teach us to connect mind with body, to learn conscious mastery over the meat-sacks we live in and through in this world. Turning an otherwise petty little life into be-here-now awareness.

The teacher is implying that where the body ends is a matter requiring debate.

I am vehement: it is beyond question where my body ends, and the rest of the world begins. You can see the boundary right there at the end of my toes – which I can now touch!

Why, she presses me, are you so proud and protective over *your* formation? What about your permeability?

I am troubled: if my boundaries are vague, if I do not belong to myself, how can I take responsibility for anything at all?

Skin can be pierced. Wounds may heal, or not. A boundary shifts. When we bleed, a little bit of the inside meets the outside and a little bit of outside rushes in. Skin absorbs and discharges moisture, swells or shrinks in response to temperature and humidity variation. Bodies change shape, size, and composition multiple times over entire lives. Humans swap zillions of electrons with their environments, and other living creatures, every second of every day.

Ninety-nine per cent of the human body is made up of atoms of hydrogen, carbon, nitrogen and oxygen. These basic compounds comprise everything that exists.

How separate is each body from every other thing, really? If we zoom in, we might see that every boundary is simply an idea.

Flo

I am in mourning still, for our dog, who died only four months ago. He was a beach mutt who adopted us one holiday morning when we had gone for a run. He came all the way up the beach and swam over the river, impressing us with his youthful vim, though we later learned he had likely been already quite old. We discovered he had been abandoned by his former humans when they went back to Europe. The campsite managers were threatening to send him to the SPCA in Mthatha, where he would surely be euthanised. After he hammily curled up on our stuff when we were packing the car to leave, we let him climb in and took him with us. He quickly became the centre of our small family, even though we'd both "never wanted a dog".

Four years later, we had to put him down after an arduous week of waiting to see if the doggy-chemotherapy pills worked and manually catheterising him twice a day to empty his bladder. The tumour was pressing closed his urethra. Because peeing on stuff during walks is one of the activities that brings a dog joy, and the tumour was going nowhere, the vets said we had no option but to let him go.

After he left us, a series of quite serious things happened that caused damage (a mugging, injuries, an emergency surgery, Covid, chronic insomnia), and it dawned on me that he had protected and patrolled the perimeter of my life in a more fundamental way than I had ever realised. Perhaps he was *never* barking at *nothing*.

Since losing Captain, I try to fill the dog-shaped hole in my life by petting whichever dog will let me when I come across them.

I arrive at the wine farm next door and announce myself to the first person I see, a worker hosing down some outdoor furniture. He goes to fetch someone in charge, and two hounds rush protectively out of a building with them. I bend down to greet the dogs, and they both immediately dissolve into wags. I ruffle one soft orange head. Her owner says, "Oh yeah Flo will go with you," when I ask if he minds if I take a little walk around their property. So, after I bury my hands in her shoulder fur and she collapses to show me her belly, we head up the paved road under the old oak trees circled by giant delicious monsters. Flo bounds along happily. Attracted by a rustle in the dead leaves, she stands at attention, eyes riveted on a spot. I follow her example when I hear a rustle of my own, and there to reward me is a skinny, black snake sticking her pretty head out to get some sun. I follow a flash of red to notice a cardinal woodpecker fly to a thick bough and commence knock-knock-knocking. Flo is beautifully alive. Her smile and wet nose take me up to see the vines past the stream chuckling down the mountain. She disappears to explore some smell, and I figure she knows the way better than I, so turn back without her. The path feels emptier for it, but she comes racing down before too long to catch up with me, and then wades into the pond for a swim. I wave goodbye at the worker near the outbuilding, so they'll know I've left, and Flo accompanies me down to the gate. I ask her to sit, and she does. I ask her to stay, and she does. I pat her warm head and tell her, with all my heart, that she is a very, very, very good dog. I turn back at the last bend, and see her still sitting there politely, watching me go.

RatHeart-LoveSong

Nicole Thackwray

Waste a while in your own chest
Until the harvest of your heart
Becomes unfamiliar to you.
Your inelastic aorta,
Blue cobweb palms.
The sag of the belly,
Blessing of softness.

Could you be a thing with a thousand hearts
A ship of Theseus
Vessel for blood and marrow,
The center of your sails
Turned inward to face themselves
Regrow and knit.
Halfmotions, become dull imprints
Or quiet aches.
Why so yielding?
Why so yielding?

But there, in the thick of me,
I knew you once.
Dreadfooted and pumping,
You did not know taming.
Sublingual,

Dissolved under my language.
In a nightmarket trade –
My voice for three pearls,
Woad-blue and pitted
In that plastic oyster.

I was not brave enough
To look into you when you came.
Pushed in, basketless,
On a granated and viscous tide.

In waking dreams
I prophesy what I would have found there,
Like a bleeding oracle.
Were you
CurledUp,
ClosedEye,
SoftPaw?
Viscera split and spilled for the short-bladed haruspex
To have cross-section of your heart?

You did not return to the earth
Soul surrendered, instead, to the water.
But you deserved your red-dirt
Country of birth
Country of burial.

And I would do it again if I could.
Gather safflower, wormwood, yarrow,
Spread your little limbs like coral,
Cover you in sea-clay,
Hitch you to the wings of fish.

You did not abandon ship,
I buried you at sea.
Scrabbling, wildling,
RatHeart.

lab rat

Jarred Thompson

you are placed in a cage and
injected with a fluid that races
into your left ventricle.
shockwaves fractal in the
intersitial fluid and suddenly,
a difference in pressure
ruptures sense.
this is not the first time.
many hands have held you,
stroked you, pinched your
skin. the scars are there.
stiff. resistant to being
anything but a strangle.
then comes the heart attack
again. you don't know why you suffer.
why being penetrated
by sharp instruments
is turning you solid.
when the medicine is given
it hurts, like before,
and though you do not know it,
this is your cross-link, the wad of bubble-gum

chewed on by another, worked into a substance
that gives as much as it says *no.*
this isn't a cure, but it will buy time
enough before the next injectate. take succour.
without you an entire alien civilisation
would stir themselves into pure simulation.
at least with you—induced, revived, reorganised—
they get to feel a pulse quicken, before its inevitable slack.
with you they get to look back in the mirror
and trace evidence of their suffering.
The hope of a different direction.

19

An Interplay with Flow

Mehita Iqani and Wamuwi Mbao

It is probably there, in that space of interplay that the relations of ideology to the sciences are established. The hold of ideology over scientific discourse and the ideological functioning of the sciences are not articulated at the level of their ideal structure (even if they can be expressed in it in a more or less visible way), nor at the level of their technical use in a society (although that society may obtain results from it), nor at the level of the consciousness of the subjects that built it up; they are articulated where science is articulated upon knowledge.
(Michel Foucault, *The Archaeology of Knowledge*. 1969, p. 204).

The practice and theory of science communication can take many forms. One of them, which this volume represents, explores what forms of knowledge might be constructed when creative writing encounters science. Working outwards from a theoretical framework that sees the sciences as discourses constructed by human endeavour through forms of language and practices of authority, it becomes possible to ask what forms of writing might emerge through scientific encounters. This is not so much a question of genre as it is a question about the relationship between creativity and scientific experiment, between the languages deployed by scientists in their experiments and analyses and the languages forged by creatives in their ongoing efforts to understand the human condition.

FicSci is a "space of interplay"; an experimental workshop that explores what kinds of creative writing might emerge if writers are brought together with a scientist. Our starting point was the idea that each scientific discipline, including those in hermeneutic domains, has a specific way of constructing knowledge through pedagogy and research. This is inevitably ideological, to some extent or another, as Foucault demonstrates. Scientists become trained in those modes of specialist communication, which are inherently exclusionary, and which usually serve certain structures of power or strategies of empowerment. The ethic motivating the FicSci encounter works against the notion of scientific exceptionalism, where scientists are positioned as all-knowing experts who deign to 'explain' their knowledge to lesser mortals. Instead, scientists and their knowledge are positioned as resources for creative writers to think with, and vice versa. The flow of exchange goes in both directions as it might not be often that scientists get to interact with the minds of creative writers, either. The siloing of knowledge creation means that those who work in any speciality all too often lack opportunities for engagement and exchange across disciplinary discourses. FicSci offers a break from the boundary work that a lot of scientific discourse enacts and invites writerly responses to the communication of scientific findings.

In this regard, the first episode of this project, FicSci 01, brought eleven creative writers together with a biomechanical engineer. The programme was unstructured, the goals intentionally undefined.

The fourteen people whose words appear in this volume spent only three days together, in a quiet valley in the Cape Winelands, nourished by delicious food and buoyed by wonderful views, soundtracked by the wind and the distant barks of dogs and baboons down the valley.

Three provocations were offered by our invited scientist, Prof. Malebogo Ngoepe, a biomechanical engineer who specialises in fluid mechanics.

In her first provocation, she summarised cutting edge research into the computational modelling of blood clots aimed at treating brain aneurysms.

In her second provocation, she explained her research into the structure and properties of hair fibres, especially the varieties common among Black African people, which is aimed at learning more about strength, plasticity, and hydrogen bonding.

In her third provocation, she presented new heart attack therapies being explored, which are testing the possibilities of hydrogels in carrying regenerative stem cell tissue to hearts damaged by cardiac disease.

All three provocations explored novel enquiry into different aspects of *flow*, that physical property that is so central to research in fluid mechanics.

The gathered writers listened, questioned, discussed, and debated. And then, we wrote. Midway through, we had a session where we shared thoughts about what to write. We chatted and philosophised over meals or walks. We played board games and stoked the fire. But mostly, we sat quietly on our own or in company in the common area. And wrote. No writer could leave the workshop without emailing the convenors a draft of something. No rules or requirements were set about what to write, in which language, or with which genre or topic to conform. Writers were to write whatever they wanted, to respond in words to whatever about the science had moved them, to concretise somehow in their genre or experimental form of choice whatever themes, ideas, metaphors or meanings the interactions with the scientist sparked in them.

The result is this anthology. It has been created in the spirit of interdisciplinary exchange and experimental writing, and comes from a genuine, and delightful, encounter.

From the scientist's presentation, various themes were taken up by the writers, ranging from magical and sci-fi screen-ready seed-narratives, to deep ancestral conversations with grandparents, and those that came long before. The cavernous symbolisms of blood, body parts, and hair types show up again and again in the pieces assembled here, as do various senses of motion, journey and movement through space (and indeed time). We have organised the pieces in the form of a journey from the metaphysical realm of spiritual callings to the workaday context of the laboratory workbench, transcending the embodied, bleeding fleshiness of bodies and traversing through urban and rural landscapes, along the way. But, of course, there will be other bridges and pathways that connect the pieces of writing. We hope that readers will also feel free to jump around, read backwards, pick up things at random, or dip in and out depending on the mood and interest that moves them at time of reading.

Busisiwe Mahlangu's short story takes us to the moment a granddaughter, seeing her beloved grandmother's body just before the burial, realises that she must follow a spiritual path. Here, blood takes on all the complex metaphysical and spiritual meanings that animate many indigenous cultures around the world.

Deepening this theme, Vuyokazi Ngemntu assembles a lyrical and fiery commentary on ancestral trauma and divination, and the multiple meanings of blood as both life force and tangible set of ties that bind across space and time, between the material and the spiritual.

Fezeka Mkhabela offers us evocative notes towards an epic Afro-fantasy novel: entwined in metaphors of ancestry and spiritual power as coded in blood and hair, we meet a magical heroine who seeks peace and justice for an ancient wrong committed.

Luyolo Vukaza's short story in isiXhosa, which we offer untranslated because we wish to honour the language and avoid any suggestion that vernacular literature must be transformed into English to be valued and published, takes us to the deathbed of a sick woman who has been painfully excluded from the social life of her village.

The physical properties of hair – its tensility and strength, its coil and kink – unearthed some marvellous narrative explorations. Jarred Thompson offers a spectacular triptych poem with vignettes of the kinds of intimacy that are produced when one person touches the hair of another.

Sithembiso Khaliswayo also fixates on the properties of hair, imagining supernatural powers attached to different hair conditions, and a giving us glimpses into a terrifying society where children with different hair (and supernatural abilities) are locked away for reform.

Some writers mused on the aneurysm in poetic form. Jarred Thompson offers a tribute to the mysteries of the never discovered blood clot. Nicole Thackwray jumped at the opportunity to go within, imagining a haemophiliac struggling with the paradox of learning they host a possibly harmless, possibly deadly aneurysm. The screenplay – or mindplay, as Thackwray re-thinks the genre – takes the reader on a journey into questions of mortality, health and indeed the sense of self that is challenged when illness looms. But the piece also considers the ontological status of the aneurysm itself, giving it voice and character.

The subject of blood transported a few writers, the materiality of bleeding taking them into the realms of violence and injury. Zanta Nkumane thinks about blood and injury in relation to broken hearts and drunken self-harm, in a piece that might be autobiographical to the extent that it explores something most are sure to feel as part of being human. Jerome Coetzee's poems sit with the psychic traces of violence that are connoted when the body and its functions, its integrity, its implied survival and safety, are systemically violated. Wamuwi Mbao ruminates on famous, and not so famous, deaths and near-deaths and ways of staying alive: the body-becoming-thing.

Alastair Mackay's short story draws on metaphors of blood and flow, transposing them on to a city at night, as a Joburg Uber driver delivers his passengers – some benign, others threatening – from one location to the next. His movements through the arteries of that difficult city are shadowed by his own traumas of migration and violence.

Mika Conradie gathers the mechanics and metaphors of fluidity into some mnemonic meditations on the river in a narrator's childhood small town, bringing together moving questions of ancestry, familial love, and belonging. Staying with the environmental, Alistair Mackay's poem pushes one of the metaphors deployed in his short story – which compares blood with resin – further, as he contemplates what binds human beings and trees. Mehita Iqani also considers space and belonging through notes on boundaries and connections, evoking questions of what divides each "I" from other forms of being.

More than one writer was moved by the plight of the lab rat, and how its tissues are used in experiments to better understand the behaviours of fluids injected into the human heart. Jarred Thompson and Nicole Thackwray offer poetic odes to this humble (yet intelligent, resilient) creature alongside whom we have evolved, and to whom we owe so much in terms of scientific discovery and understanding. With this humble chunk of minced lab rat meat, from which so much knowledge can be gleaned, the collection closes.

Please remember that the pieces published here were written quite quickly, and though they were developed somewhat in the time after the workshop, they are true to the form that each had taken by the end of the three-day experience. Writers were carefully selected to include a range of voices, backgrounds and styles. This comes through in the diversity of the pieces included in this collection. Although very diverse in style, tone and experimentation with genre, the collection is united by the real creative engagement that all the writers showed with the science presented to them. These pieces are offered in the spirit of flash fiction, which prioritises the presentation of prompts and provocations to turn the spotlight on intensive experimental writing. Varyingly imperfect, by turns muted or jarring or poetic, they each in their own way use science to story the world.

It is somewhat difficult to give one label to the multiple genres of writing that this collection includes. These range from poetry to short stories, from screen plays to experimental essays. The contents of this volume are neither science journalism nor science-fiction; they are certainly not press releases for a lab or notes to assist in a classroom. They cannot serve a pedagogical or explicatory goal and will not help the reader to understand any of the complexities of fluid mechanics and biomedical engineering. And yet, they do something with, and perhaps to, the data presented by Prof.

Ngoepe. They teach us, in the way that only literary material can, by engaging the creative and narrative aspects of intelligence, by exploring the humanist aspects of the world in which the science operates. The pieces included in this collection explore some of the questions and puzzles with which the science they were exposed to is concerned. This happens sometimes metaphorically in ways that explore various aspects of the human condition, for with what else but the human condition can science ever be said to be concerned? The works gathered here are also quite different from the kinds of free-writing pieces that might emerge from simple writing prompts, because the presentations offered by Prof. Ngoepe rather than being merely writing prompts, were detailed presentations of leading-edge scientific thought. The writers engaged with the material with their writerly brains, following leads and considering pathways of meaning. They brought the human into the science, which is the unique contribution that creative modalities of thinking and exploring can offer the collaborative project of constructing knowledge. By bringing the practices and discourses of creative writing and literary endeavour into direct contact with science, and vice versa, FicSci has offered a new pathway for thinking about interdisciplinary exchange.

The FicSci 01 anthology is the first product of an encounter between fiction and science in the South African literary landscape. It offers a record of a space of interplay between fluid biomechanics research and creative writing, and through this challenges the boundaries that exist between various forms of knowledge creation.

Biographies

Alistair Mackay writes fiction and non-fiction that explores queer-ness, marginalisation, social justice and climate change. He has been published in a number of South African media titles, such as the *Financial Mail* and *Daily Maverick*, and was a regular columnist for *Mambaonline* and *MarkLives*. His debut novel, *It Doesn't Have To Be This Way*, was chosen by Brittle Paper and *Mail & Guardian* as one of their Notable African Books of 2022, and was long-listed for the British Science Fiction Association Awards in 2023. His second novel, *The Child*, is forthcoming from Kwela in 2024. Alistair's short stories have been published in *New Contrast*, Brittle Paper, Commonwealth Writers' *Adda Magazine*, *The Kalahari Review*, and in the anthologies *Queer Africa: Selected Stories*, and *Queer Africa II*, which was a finalist in the 2018 Lambda Literary Awards. Born and raised in Johannesburg, he currently lives in Cape Town. He holds an MA in Politics from Edinburgh University and an MFA in Creative Writing from Columbia University. For more information, visit www.alistaircharlesmackay.com

Busisiwe Mahlangu is a writer and performer from Mamelodi, Pretoria. Her debut collection, *Surviving Loss* (2018), was adapted for theatre. She was a fellow at the Johannesburg Institute for Advanced Study (2022), working on her second poetry manuscript, *A Body Makes Fire*. She has performed all over South Africa and has shared her work on international stages including Lesotho, Mozambique, Sweden, Nigeria and the USA. Mahlangu was awarded the inaugural SA National Poetry Prize by *New Contrast* in 2020. Her work has been long-listed for the Sol Plaatje European Poetry Award and published in *The Kalahari Review*, *Ja* magazine, *Best 'New' African Poets*, *Atlanta Review*, *Yesterdays and Imagining Realities*, *Wild Imperfections* and elsewhere. She holds a BA in Creative Writing from the University of South Africa. When she is not writing, she makes beaded jewellery and accessories under 'Busi Creates'. For more information, visit busimahlangu.com

Fezeka Mkhabela is a writer, producer and documentary filmmaker whose work is influenced by a call to illuminate African knowledge systems and cultural practices through the moving image. Fezeka holds an honour's degree in Film and Television Production with a specialisation in Screenwriting and Performance Theory from the University of the Witwatersrand. In 2021, she founded Ingwe Studios, a production studio company that champions indigenous storytelling through the visual medium. She is an alumnus of the IsiZulu Scriptwriting Masterclass held during the Durban International Film Festival and the emerging filmmaker's programme held by the Pan African Film Festival of Ouagadougou. Her creative writing has seen publication in *Tint Journal Austria* and *The Culture Review South Africa*. For more information, visit www.iamfezeka.com

Jarred Thompson is a literary and cultural studies researcher and educator, and works as a lecturer in the English Department at the University of Pretoria. He was the winner of the 2020 Afritondo Prize and the runner-up in the 2021 Dream Foundry Prize. His debut novel, *The Institute for Creative Dying*, is published through Picador Africa and Afritondo UK.

Jerome Coetzee is a writer, poet, and master's candidate in the Department of Afrikaans at the University of the Western Cape. His research focus is on Afrofuturism in contemporary Afrikaans literature. He has previously been published in *LitNet*, *Die Student* and is a National Poetry Prize winner (2021). He was on the long list for the Sol Plaatje European Union Award (2022). When he is not writing, Jerome can be found at local poetry reading events with a pen and a notebook, and always with a cup of tea. In his spare time, he also enjoys mentoring and facilitating online poetry workshops.

Luyolo Vukuza is a twenty-two year-old who was raised by his aunt in a small village known as Bhibha. He and his two sisters lost their mother in 2006, when he was only five years old. His tough childhood experiences have greatly influenced his writing, which explores socio-political themes. His accolades include university competitions, which have led to the publication of his poem 'Iinkwenkwezi eziqaqambileyo'. He is currently a student at Walter Sisulu University, studying towards a Bachelor of Education (in isiXhosa and English). He has also worked at Ingwane FM as a news reader. In 2021, he joined the MCPA (Mthatha Campus Performing Arts) as a poet and later discovered his love for acting. In 2023 he was elected as the deputy-secretary of the MCPA.

Mika Conradie has produced curatorial, exhibition and editorial programming with and for Lagos Photo, Jakarta Biennale and GALA Queer Archive, amongst others. From 2016 to 2021 she co-directed POOL, a not-for-profit arts organisation in Johannesburg. Her writing on art, design and visual practice is published by K.Verlag, Transnational Dialogues, Art South Africa and Gdańska Galeria Miejska. More of her work can be found on Instagram: @soft_wave.

Nicole Thackwray is a writer, teacher and multidisciplinary artist. She is currently pursuing a postgraduate qualification in visual communication at Open Window while teaching young African creatives about the importance of art history, mirror-neurons and of three-point lighting, among other things. Her work centres on people – particularly the generational ties between women – as well as technology, the modern condition and occasionally takes surrealist rambles into nowhere. She is a recent recipient of a

National Poetry Prize (third place, 2023), and her work has been published in *New Contrast* and *Ons Klyntji*, among other publications. She lives in Gauteng with her dog and perpetually overflowing personal library. When she's not writing, she makes short films, and dreams up art installations. You can follow her on Instagram @toomanynoodles, or visit her Behance profile: https://www.behance.net/190045adoba481

Sithembiso Khalishwayo is an actor, dancer, teacher, lecturer, writer, photographer, videographer, choreographer, published poet, creative researcher, activist and a facilitator who studied at the Wits School of Arts in conjunction with Drama for Life (DFL). He majored in physical theatre, performance and applied drama and holds a BA in Performing and Visual Arts and a master's degree in Applied Drama. He was the student representative chair for the DFL Student Council in 2016 during the #FeesMustFall Movement. He is the recipient of the Pieter-Dirk Uys Theatre for Social Change and the Judge Edwin Cameron Theatre for Human Rights awards, and winner of the 2015 Wits Photographic Competition. He also placed second in South Africa's PEN Student Writing competition. Currently, he supervises and trains Radio Drama Honours research students and is the project manager of the DFL Lifebeats radio show on Vowfm. He also curates the Drama for Life's Rehearse//Reveal Festival and is a senior member of the DFL Theatre Company.

Vuyokazi Ngemntu is a writer-performer located in Cape Town, South Africa, whose praxis uses poetry, song, physical theatre, storytelling and ritual to navigate ancestral trauma, confront inequality and inspire healing. Recent career highlights include having her short story 'Binnegoed' selected as the overall winner of *Ibua Journal*'s 2022 Bold: Food regional contest. Another milestone includes having her short story 'The Serpent's Handmaiden' short-listed for the Share Africa Climate Change Fiction Award. Her work has appeared or is forthcoming in *The Kalahari Review, Herri, Ibua Journal, Ake Review, The Culture Review, Short.Sharp.Stories, Aerodrome* and elsewhere.

Zanta Nkumane is a Swazi writer, journalist and ex-scientist. His work has appeared in the *Mail & Guardian*, *OkayAfrica*, *This Is Africa*, *Lolwe*, *Racebaitr*, *The Johannesburg Review of Books* and *The Republic*. He is also a Short Story Day Africa Inkubator Fellow 2022/23, the incumbent non-fiction editor at *Doek!* literary magazine and the 2022/23 UEA Booker Prize Scholar.

Editors

Mehita Iqani is an academic researcher and writer in the field of media, communications and cultural studies, in which she has published widely. She is currently based in the Journalism Department at Stellenbosch University where she runs research projects on climate and environment, health and happiness, and creative communications through the DSI-NRF-funded SA Research Chair in Science Communication, of which she is chairholder.

Wamuwi Mbao is a writer and literary critic. He teaches literature at Stellenbosch University. His research interests are in South African popular culture, literary criticism, and architecture and automotive histories. He is the editor of *Years of Fire and Ash: South African Poetry of Decolonization*. He is a fiction critic with *The Johannesburg Review of Books* and poetry editor at *New Contrast*. His work has appeared in various publications. His short story 'The Bath' was noted as one of the most significant short stories of South Africa's new democracy. He is the recipient of a South African Literary Award for his body of literary criticism.

Invited scientist

Malebogo Ngoepe is a mechanical engineer interested in the role of mechanics in health and disease. Her work in biomechanics covers topics in blood clotting, children's heart disease and curly hair. She is an Associate-Professor in the Department of Mechanical Engineering at the University of Cape Town, and directs the Centre for Research in Computational and Applied Mechanics.

www.ingramcontent.com/pod-product-compliance
Lightning Source LLC
Chambersburg PA
CBHW040149270326
41929CB00025B/3437